CW00485066

The XXL Air Fryer Cookbook

UK 2023

Affordable, Mouthwatering, and Super-Amazing

Air Fryer Recipes for Everyday Enjoyment

including Inspirations for

Breakfast, Lunch, Dinner, Desserts & More

Anna C. Walker

Copyright © [2022] [Anna C. Walker]

All rights reserved

The author of this book owns the exclusive right to its content. Any commercial usage or reproduction requires the clear consent of the author.

ISBN - 9798363211348

Table of Contents

EXCLUSIVE BONUS

40 Weight Loss Recipes

&

14 Days Meal Plan

Scan the QR-Code and receive
the FREE download:

Introduction

If you have an air fryer, you are probably always looking for new ways to use your device to make delicious, crispy, and healthy food for the whole family, no matter what time of day or what day of the week. Fortunately, air fryers are versatile and allow you to make all kinds of meals – not just chips / fries!

It's a great idea to use your air fryer regularly so you can make the most of the gadget and the health boost it offers. To be clear before starting, food is not automatically healthy just because it has been cooked in an air fryer. It often still contains quite a high level of fat, and many air fryer foods (e.g., chips / fries, waffles, bacon, doughnuts, steaks, and more) are not particularly healthy. However, using an air fryer is much better for you than deep frying your meals, so if you're a fan of fried meals, it's definitely a better option because it will massively reduce the amount of oil that is in your food.

This can have major health benefits and is an ideal option if you are struggling to reduce your dependence on fried foods. Instead of soaking your foods in oil, you can enjoy the same crispy, delightful coating on the exterior, and a much lower fat count overall. Air fryers are definitely the best way to make your favourite foods healthier and more diet- friendly, so let's learn a bit more about them!

All About Air Fryers

If you don't yet own an air fryer but you're thinking of getting one (or if you do own one but you aren't quite sure how this amazing gadget works), it's best to think of an air fryer as a mini convection oven with superpowers. It isn't actually frying your food – what it does is closer to baking it, but the resulting taste and texture are very much like fried food.

Air fryers are known for being amazingly versatile, and they also cook quickly. They have seen an enormous uptake in recent years, and you can cook a whole range of foods in an air fryer, including frozen meat without needing to defrost it, and even things like cookies. Given how flexible they are, it's hardly surprising that so many people are keen to try these gadgets out.

To give a quick overview of just how versatile an air fryer is, the food categories you can cook in them include:

- Some baked goods
- Meat and fish
- Roasted vegetables
- Frozen finger foods
- Homemade finger foods

Almost anything can be made in an air fryer, although not absolutely everything can – so find a good recipe before you test this theory!

What Are the Pros of Air Fryers?

There are a lot of advantages to using these cookers, but the biggest thing is the reduction in oil. It's thought that using an air fryer can often result in about a third of the oil use, depending on the approach and the food being cooked. If you are trying to cut back on oil, this is an amazing way to do it, without compromising on the taste and texture.

Another major advantage is the speed. Air fryers tend to cook food quickly, so you can have a finished meal on the table in a very short amount of time, which is ideal if you are feeding kids or working long hours (or both). They are also a great way to cook meat from frozen; if you have forgotten to thaw chicken or another meat before leaving the house for the day, you don't need to muck around with the microwave or cold water before cooking it. Air fryers get up to temperature fast enough to safely cook frozen meat.

Air fryers also tend to be reasonably cheap to buy and will represent a major financial saving in oil if you regularly make fried foods. There are plenty of other reasons to use them, but these are the major advantages offered by this kind of cooker.

What Are the Cons Of Air Fryers?

Of course, no cooker is perfect, and an air fryer does have some drawbacks. One of the biggest is its capacity. Because they are counter- top machines, even a large air fryer can only make a relatively small amount of food at one time, and that means you have to cook food in batches. Because fried food needs to be eaten hot, this can be annoying, especially if you are feeding a lot of people. However, it is also often a problem when deep frying the traditional way, unless you have an industrial fryer, so it isn't a deal breaker in most cases.

Another issue with air fryers is that they do still use quite a bit of oil for food. It's massively reduced, but you can't cook without oil, so you will still be incorporating it into your diet regularly. It's also very easy to burn food in an air fryer, because of the high temperatures involved. You need to be hands-on and alert when cooking using this gadget, or it could ruin your dinner or even present a danger.

Air Fryer Use and Maintenance

If you've never used an air fryer before, it's important to point out that this is generally a very simple process. You will usually be brushing or spraying the food with oil, setting the temperature and time on your device, and then allowing the food to cook. This will usually take between 5 minutes and half an hour, depending on the foods you are making. Sometimes, you will need to turn the food halfway through, and at other times, you can just leave it to cook.

Of course, you need to maintain your air fryer if it is going to produce delicious foods for you; like all forms of cookers, it will need cleaning and caring for. Many people underestimate the maintenance involved when they first get an air fryer and feel frustrated by this once they own one.

So, how do you look after your air fryer? Well, firstly, you need to let the whole thing cool down and then unplug it. Next, clean the basket, pan, and tray after every use, just as you would any cooking utensil. Some air fryers have dishwasher-safe components, while others will need to be hand-washed. In general, handwashing is preferable because it will help these components to last longer.

Wash the utensils in hot, soapy water, using a soft cloth. If any bits of food are stuck on, soak the component for a while to loosen it and then have another go. Never use metal tools, wire wool, abrasive brushes, or any other tough scrubbers to get stuck residue off the components. This will scratch the non-stick coating and could permanently ruin that part of the equipment. Always be gentle when cleaning these parts.

You should also wipe out the inside of the air fryer with a damp, slightly soapy cloth to remove any residue. Be careful not to get the main part of the machine wet, however, because it is electric, and this will destroy it. A damp cloth, followed by a thorough dry with a towel will be sufficient to keep the interior clean. Never put the main air fryer in the sink or the dishwasher.

What Is Air Fryer Food Like?

Air fryer food is actually closer to baked food in terms of how it is made, but it is very much like fried food, although slightly less greasy. Because of the coating of oil and the hot temperature, the food develops a deliciously crispy, satisfying coating on the outside, while remaining tender and succulent inside. Meat cooked in an air fryer will remain tender and chewy in the middle, but it will take on that deliciously crunchy exterior that is usually only found in deep fried foods.

That has made air fryer food enormously popular; it hits the craving for fat, retains the texture and juiciness of meat, and is better for you than normal fried food. It's ideal when you want something greasy and satisfying, but if you fancy something healthier, remember that you can also air fry vegetables. These will be akin to tender roasted vegetables, and they make an ideal side to a roast dinner.

Air fryer food is therefore a delicious option, and many people really enjoy eating it. However, if you aren't a fan of fried food overall, you will likely find that it's too greasy for you – even if the oil has been massively reduced compared with regular fried food!

What Common Mistakes Do People Make When Using an Air Fryer?

Before we start looking at some actual recipes, let's learn a bit about the commonest air fryer mistakes that people tend to make when they are using an air fryer. Understanding these in advance will help to ensure that you avoid them, meaning your food will taste better and your appliance will last longer!

- Don't put too much oil on your foods. Although many of us think of oil as adding that delicious taste and this might be a hard habit to break initially, putting a lot of oil on your foods will actually ruin them when you are using an air fryer. They will take on a greasy, heavy texture, and will turn limp rather than crispy. A light coating is often enough, and you can always add a second coating when you check on the food later if you decide it isn't getting enough crispiness.

- Don't forget to preheat your air fryer. Like getting the oil in the pan hot before you add your food, it's crucial to toss the food into a hot environment so that the outside crisps up immediately. Failure to do this will result in soggy food that just never takes on that mouth-watering crispy coating. Always preheat your air fryer; this shouldn't take long and makes an enormous difference to the meal.

- Take some time to learn which foods don't work well in an air fryer. When you get a shiny new kitchen gadget, it's always tempting to throw anything and everything into it to see what happens. Air fryers might be great, but they are not all-powerful. Foods need to be a certain weight in order to work in an air fryer, or they will simply get blown about by the fan and won't cook properly. If you want to cook things like kale or tortillas in your air fryer, you'll need to weigh them down with other ingredients to stop them simply flying around in the basket.

- Always make sure you are using the right oil. It might not seem like it would make a difference, but remember that the oil's smoke point is important, especially when you are cooking at high temperatures (which air fryers always are). If you choose an oil with a low smoke point, such as coconut oil or canola oil, your food will burn. It will taste awful, and it's thought that the carcinogens that are created could be really bad for you.

You should always be cooking with an oil that has a higher temperature than your cooking temperature. An air fryer's maximum temperature is usually around 480 degrees F, and that means it's crucial to choose an oil with a high smoke point, such as sunflower oil (486 degrees F), avocado oil (520 degrees F), peanut oil (440 degrees F), or sesame oil (450 degrees F). If you are cooking at a lower temperature, it may be okay to use a lower smoke point oil, but always check that your oil's smoke point is at least a few degrees higher than the hottest cooking temperature.

- Don't neglect to check on the food, either. Some cooking methods (e.g., ovens, slow cookers) lose a lot of heat when you open them to check on the food, so this tends to be discouraged. However, with air fryers, you can let this habit die, because they won't lose notable amounts of heat when you take the food out, and air fried food often benefits from being turned, tossed, or re-oiled while it is cooking. Don't just set the timer and walk away.

- Don't overfill your air fryer's basket. It might be tempting if you are trying to cram enough food in there for your whole family to enjoy, but it simply will not work well. If the hot air cannot circulate around the food, it will not form a crispy coating. Instead, you will get uneven cooking, with some parts burning while other parts are still soft or even cold. Make sure you only fill the basket to its maximum quantity and allow air to circulate over all of the food. If this means cooking in batches, that's unfortunately your only option, because stuffing the basket will not work.

- Don't be afraid to experiment with new foods. Hopefully, this book is going to counteract this tendency anyway, but some people only use their air fryers for the standard fried foods, such as chips / fries, bacon, and chicken nuggets. However, an air fryer can make so many foods, it is absolutely worth using your air fryer to experiment and vary your diet. Don't limit yourself before you have even started!

- Remember to clean your air fryer regularly. We already touched on cleaning the air fryer after every use, but you should also do the occasional deep clean to remove any built-up residue. To achieve this, you will need to unplug and cool the air fryer, and then wipe it and clean it as mentioned above. Next, use a toothpick or a dedicated toothbrush (dry) to scrub out the insides and get into all the nooks and crannies. If crumbs of food build up in these areas, they will start to burn the next time you turn the fryer on, and this could ruin the taste of your new food, as well as create an awful, acrid smell. Knock out the crumbs and turn the air fryer over if necessary to get to all the different parts.

Make sure the air fryer is completely dry before you reassemble its parts. Never put wet components back into the machine, as this could be dangerous. Dry all the parts and allow any remaining moisture to air dry off them before putting everything back together.

If you follow these simple instructions, you should find that your air fryer cooking journey is smooth and straightforward! Keep your air fryer clean and keep experimenting with new recipes, and you'll find this gadget is a joy to have in your kitchen.

Great Air Fryer Recipes for Breakfast

An air fryer is often whipped out for making a tasty dinner, but what about breakfast? This meal is sometimes rushed and neglected, but it doesn't have to be. Your air fryer can make you amazing breakfast options on any day of the week, and it's a wonderfully quick, low-mess way to enjoy a fry-up.

Air Fried Hash Browns

Do you love hash browns? They are a great way to start the day, as potato is filling and contains plenty of nutrients. Fortunately, they are also super easy to make in an air fryer, and they are perfect for a weekend breakfast that the whole family can enjoy. You can make these with fresh potatoes, but surprisingly, frozen shredded potatoes will actually give you much crispier hash browns because they contain a lot less moisture! If you can use frozen, do.

SERVES: 4

You will need:

450 g / 16 oz shredded potatoes (preferably frozen)
½ teaspoon of garlic powder
Salt and pepper to taste

Nutrition Info:
Calories: 79 | Fat: 0.1 g | Cholesterol: 0 mg
Sodium: 46 mg | Carbohydrates: 18.1 g | Fibre: 2.8 g | Protein: 2 g

Method:

1. Start by preheating your air fryer until it reaches 185 degrees C / 370 degrees F.
2. Open your bag of frozen potatoes (or shred your potatoes and drain as much liquid off them if you can if you don't have frozen potatoes) and weigh out the right amount. Tip this into your air fryer basket and then spray it with olive oil and sprinkle it with salt, pepper, and garlic powder. You can bump up the garlic powder if you like.
3. Cook the potatoes for about 18 or 19 minutes, checking on them occasionally. When they are starting to turn golden on top, use a wooden spatula to divide the portion up into four sections. Next, carefully flip them over.
4. Put them back into the air fryer and allow them to fry for another 5 minutes, or until they are as golden as you enjoy them.
5. Serve hot.

Air Fried Crispy Bacon and Eggs

Everybody loves bacon and eggs; they make the perfect breakfast treat, but it can be a pain to make in a pan. Bacon spits and hisses and splatters oil all over the place, so why not try making it in your air fryer? This is a brilliant way to enjoy your bacon and eggs, and it makes cooking so simple! You can even toss some toast in with it if you like, so the whole meal is made as one.

SERVES: 1

You will need:

> 2 eggs
> 2 strips of bacon
> 1 teaspoon of butter
> 2 slices of bread

Nutrition Info:
> Calories: 430 | Fat: 30.2 g | Cholesterol: 424 mg | Sodium: 1167 mg
> Carbohydrates: 10.4 g | Fibre: 0.4 g | Protein: 21.8 g

Method:

1. Take your slices of bread and lightly butter them. Put them in the air fryer basket with the butter facing down.
2. Cut your bacon slices in half. Take one slice per piece of bread and curl the two halves to make a cup in the middle of the slice of bread. This will create a ring that holds the egg in the centre and prevents it from slipping down through the basket.
3. Crack the first egg onto the first piece of bread and the second onto the second piece of bread, inside the bacon rings you have created.
4. Place the basket inside the air fryer and cook it at 180 degrees C / 350 degrees F for around eight minutes, until the eggs have set, and the bacon is crispy. Serve hot.

Asparagus And Egg Air Fryer Croquettes

If you love croquettes, these asparagus and egg ones will really hit the spot for you. They are a little more involved in terms of a breakfast meal, but well worth the extra work. However, be aware of the chilling time needed, and don't try to make these if you are rushing to get to work or starting a busy day, or you'll end up late.

SERVES: 6

You will need:

9 large eggs

25 g / ½ cup of spring onion / green onion

3 tablespoons of plain / all-purpose flour

3 tablespoons of butter

180 ml / ¾ cup of 2% milk

65 g / ½ cup of asparagus

75 g / 1/3 cup of cheese

210 g / 1 ¾ cups of breadcrumbs

Salt and pepper to taste

1 tablespoon of tarragon

Nutritional info:

Calories: 335 | Fat: 17.1 g | Cholesterol: 281 mg | Sodium: 520 mg
Carbohydrates: 29 g | Fibre: 2 g | Protein: 16.4 g

Method:

1. Hard boil 6 of the eggs and then plunge them into cold water and peel them.
2. Add your butter to a large saucepan and stir it over a medium heat until fully melted. Once it has melted, slowly sprinkle in the flour and stir until smooth, and then fry gently until it turns lightly golden.
3. Remove the pan from the heat and slowly add the milk, whisking well to prevent the flour from turning lumpy. Put it back over the heat and cook for a few more minutes, stirring occasionally, until the roux thickens into a white sauce.
4. Chop the hard-boiled eggs into slices. Chop the onions and raw asparagus, shred the cheese, and mince the tarragon.
5. Stir these into your white sauce, along with salt and pepper to taste, and then transfer the mixture to a bowl and allow it to cool to room temperature. Once it has cooled, put it in the fridge for at least 2 hours.
6. When the mixture is ready, preheat your air fryer to 175 degrees C / 350 degrees F. Scoop your egg mixture into twelve equal portions and shape them into 3-inch-long cylinders.
7. Tip your breadcrumbs into a bowl and roll the cylinders in them. Next, break your remaining three eggs into a separate bowl, dip each cylinder in the egg wash and roll it in breadcrumbs again. This should ensure that each croquette has a good coating of crumbs. Pat more crumbs onto any spots that haven't got properly covered.
8. Grease your air fryer basket with cooking spray. Place a single layer of croquettes in the bottom of your air fryer basket and add a little more cooking spray. Cook for around 9 minutes, until they have turned golden brown all over. Turn them over, add a little more cooking spray if necessary, and then cook for another 3-5 minutes until fully gold all over. Serve hot and start the next batch.

Veg And Bacon Sweet Potato Skins

If you are looking for a more unusual breakfast, you might love these vegetable and bacon sweet potato skins. The air fryer makes the vegetables deliciously crispy and rich, and the sweet potato skins are a perfect start to the day, with a lovely earthy flavour. Cooked in the air fryer, the skins become crunchy and tempting. You can easily swap the sweet potatoes for yams if you prefer or if that's what you have available. You can also turn this recipe into a vegetarian option if you like by omitting the bacon or using a vegetarian or vegan substitute. Swap the whole milk for plant milk, and this can be a great vegan-friendly breakfast.

SERVES: 4

You will need:

1 small tomato

4 eggs

2 teaspoons of olive oil

2 sweet potatoes

4 slices of bacon

2 spring onions / green onions

½ red bell pepper

Salt and pepper to taste

60 ml / ¼ cup of whole milk

Nutritional info:

Calories: 234 | Fat: 13.6 g | Cholesterol: 182 ml | Sodium: 437 mg
Carbohydrates: 15.3 g | Fibre: 2.5 g | Protein: 13.2 g

Method:

1. Start by scrubbing your sweet potatoes and then make some slits in their skins, across the length. Place them in the microwave for about 7 minutes. You want them to be soft, so microwave them for longer if necessary.

2. While the potatoes are microwaving, cook the bacon and chop up the tomato, onion, and red pepper.

3. Slice the potatoes lengthwise (use a towel to protect your hands as the potatoes will be very hot and may release a lot of steam). Scoop the flesh out, leaving a little around the edges, and set the flesh aside. You won't be using it in this recipe, but it can be used to create sweet potato and carrot mash, or for other purposes.

4. Brush the potato skins with olive oil and a little salt, and then put them in your air fryer basket and cook them for 10 minutes at 400 degrees F.

5. Get a non-stick skillet and warm it over a low-medium heat, and then add the milk, eggs, pepper, and salt. Stir gently and keep cooking until the egg has turned completely firm.

6. Take the potato skins out of the air fryer and add ¼ of your mixture, plus some crumbled bacon, to each skin. Put the skin back into the air fryer and cook for another 3 minutes. If you want to add some cheese to this recipe, you can melt it onto the skins at this point.

7. Once cooked, sprinkle your chopped onions, tomatoes, and red pepper across them and serve hot.

Air Fried Cinnamon Toast

Do you love eating crispy cinnamon toast first thing? This is a great, simple recipe you can whip up in no time in your air fryer. It's perfect if you'd rather have a basic breakfast that's ready in minutes.

SERVES: 2

You will need:

1 tablespoon of sugar

3 tablespoons of butter

4 slices of bread

½ teaspoon of cinnamon (or more to taste)

Nutritional info:
Calories: 155 | Fat: 9.5 g | Cholesterol: 23 mg | Sodium: 232 mg
Carbohydrates: 15.9 g | Fibre: 0.8 g | Protein: 2 g

Method:

1. Preheat your air fryer to 200 degrees C / 400 degrees F.
2. Get a small bowl and stir together the soft butter with the cinnamon and some sugar. You can adjust the quantities to match your preferences. Mix it well so the spice and sugar are well distributed.
3. Butter your bread, spreading the butter right to the corners of the slices. Be generous so you get plenty of flavouring.
4. Place the slices of bread in the air fryer basket, with the buttered side facing up, and cook for 5 minutes.
5. Serve with fresh fruit and a little more cinnamon, or a pinch of nutmeg if you prefer.

Baked Apples in An Air Fryer

Do you love baked apples? Get a bit of fruit into your diet to start the day with this rich and creamy recipe. Kids will love it too!

SERVES: 4

You will need:

2 apples

3 teaspoons of honey

½ teaspoon of ground cinnamon

45 g / ½ cup of oats

2 tablespoons of butter

Nutritional info:

Calories: 164 | Fat: 6.6 g | Cholesterol: 15 mg | Sodium: 43 mg
Carbohydrates: 26.9 g | Fibre: 3.9 g | Protein: 1.7 g

Method:

1. Preheat your air fryer to 180 degrees C / 375 degrees F.
2. Melt your butter in a small bowl, and then cut and core your apples. Brush the butter across each half.
3. In a separate bowl, mix the remaining butter with the oats, cinnamon, and honey.
4. Place the apples in your air fryer basket, buttery side up, and spoon the mixture on top of the halves.
5. Put the apples in the air fryer and cook them for up to 15 minutes, until they have turned rich and golden.
6. Top them with some ice cream or whipped cream and serve sizzling hot.

Air Fryer Frittatas

Do you love frittatas? They make a quick and ultra-simple breakfast, and the great news is that you can add anything you like to them to make them shine. No matter what ingredients you enjoy, these can be adapted to suit it, and they will be loved by everyone in the family. They are pretty quick and easy and can be made in under an hour.

SERVES: 2

You will need:

4 large eggs
2 tablespoons of diced red bell pepper
1 green onion
60 g / ½ cup of cheddar
115 g / ¼ lb of breakfast sausage
Pinch of cayenne pepper

> **Nutritional info:**
> Calories: 475 | Fat: 34.8 g | Cholesterol: 405 mg | Sodium: 728 mg
> Carbohydrates: 10.7 g | Fibre: 1.8 g | Protein: 30.5 g

Method:

1. Start by cooking your sausages until they are completely done, and then allow them to cool a little and crumble them. Chop up the green onion and grate the cheddar cheese.
2. Preheat your air fryer to 180 degrees C / 360 degrees F.
3. Get out a large mixing bowl and add your bell pepper, cayenne pepper, onion, sausage, and eggs to it. Mix them thoroughly until they are completely combined.
4. Spray a non-stick cake tin with oil and tip the egg mixture into the tin. Place it in your air fryer and cook it until the egg sets. This should take about twenty minutes.

Custard Toast in The Air Fryer

If you're a fan of toast in the morning but you're bored of eating it with peanut butter and jam / jelly, you might be looking for something a little sweeter – and custard toast is the ideal option. You can serve this with fresh berries if you like, but it's delicious just as it is. This recipe only makes enough for 1, so make sure you're at the air fryer first, or increase the ingredients so that you can whip this up for a few more members of your household.

SERVES: 1

You will need:

140 g / 5 oz of Greek yoghurt

2 slices of bread

1 tablespoon of honey

1 egg

Nutritional info:
Calories: 282 | Fat: 7.8 g | Cholesterol: 171 mg | Sodium: 231 mg
Carbohydrates: 32.5 g | Fibre: 0.5 g | Protein: 21.3 g

Method:

1. Preheat your air fryer to 190 degrees C / 375 degrees F and get out a medium bowl.
2. Crack the egg into the bowl, add the Greek yoghurt, and whisk the two together. As you whisk, add the honey and keep mixing until totally combined.
3. Take one slice of bread and set it on the side. Use a spoon to create a large well in the centre of the slice, pressing it down so that you have a hollow of compressed bread.
4. Scoop out some of your egg mixture and use it to fill the well, being careful not to fill it so much that it spills out of the well.
5. Add any other toppings you want (such as cinnamon, nutmeg, fresh fruit, etc.) and then do the same with your other slice of bread.
6. Put both slices into your air fryer basket and put the basket in the air fryer. Bake them for 8 minutes and then check on them. The edges of the bread should be turning golden brown and starting to caramelise. If they aren't yet brown enough for your tastes, put the bread back for another couple of minutes.
7. Serve hot with additional toppings if you like.

Air Fryer Potato Pancakes

If you want to make pancakes but you don't want to mess around with a pan, batter, milk, etc., these potato pancakes might be perfect for you. They are simple and filling, and they can be made in your air fryer in less than half an hour with just a handful of ingredients. Kids and adults will love them, so they are well worth making for any simple breakfast. Because of the air fryer's cooking style, you will find that they are delightfully crispy, a little like a hash brown, without being too greasy or heavy to enjoy first thing in the morning.

SERVES: 3 (2 PANCAKES EACH)

You will need:

500 g / 2 cups of mashed potatoes

115 g / 1 cup of cheddar cheese

1 egg

70 g / 1 cup of flour

2 spring / green onions

Salt to taste

Pepper to taste

Nutritional info (per 2 pancakes):
Calories: 386 | Fat: 16.1 g | Cholesterol: 97 mg | Sodium: 674 mg
Carbohydrates: 43.3 g | Fibre: 0.8 g | Protein: 17.3 g

Method:

1. Take a medium bowl and grate in the cheddar cheese and then add the mashed potato.
2. Crack the egg into the bowl and mix it in and add the flour.
3. Thinly slice the spring / green onions and add them to the bowl and mix thoroughly. Add the salt and pepper and mix everything together.
4. Take a small piece of aluminium foil and spread it in the bottom of the air fryer basket. Lightly spray it with a little bit of oil.
5. Preheat your air fryer to 190 degrees C / 390 degrees F.
6. Take 1/6th of your mixture and shape it into a patty. Do this with all of the mixture until you have 6 potato pancakes.
7. Place them in the bottom of the air fryer basket with a little bit of space between each. You may need to work in multiple batches if your air fryer is not big enough for them all at once.
8. Cook the pancakes for 8 minutes and then take the air fryer basket out and use tongs to flip each pancake over and cook them for another 5 minutes. Take them out to check them and cook for up to 3 minutes more until you have achieved the desired level of crispiness.
9. Serve with a scoop of sour cream or tomato ketchup and enjoy.

Air Fried Omelettes

Do you love omelettes? They are super easy to make in your air fryer, so they are perfect for breakfast. It does only make one omelette at a time, so you might find you've got to work in several batches, as these are bound to be a very popular option with the whole family. You can vary the filling if you don't like any of the below suggestions; simply swap them for an alternative! If you want a vegetarian option, omit the ham and enjoy just vegetables, or a vegetarian meat substitute. Note that you will need a pan that will fit into your air fryer basket, as you can't cook raw egg directly in the basket; it will drip through the gaps.

SERVES: 1

You will need:

2 eggs
30 g / ¼ cup of ham
40 g / ¼ cup of red pepper / bell pepper
25 g / ¼ cup of spring / green onions
20 g / ¼ cup of mushrooms
½ teaspoon of thyme
½ teaspoon of chives
30 g / ¼ cup of cheddar cheese
55 g / ¼ cup of mozzarella
60 ml / ¼ cup of milk
Pinch of salt

Nutritional info:

Calories: 368 | Fat: 23.7 g | Cholesterol: 385 mg | Sodium: 971 mg
Carbohydrates: 10.6 g | Fibre: 1.9 g | Protein: 29.1 g

Method:

1. Take a medium bowl and crack the eggs into it. Beat them until they are frothy.
2. Add the milk and mix it into the eggs thoroughly.
3. Wash and chop the vegetables and chop up the ham into small pieces.
4. Mix the vegetables and ham into the omelette mixture and then grease a pan that will fit into your air fryer.
5. Preheat the air fryer to 175 degrees C / 350 degrees F and place the pan in the air fryer when it's hot. Cook the omelette for 5 minutes.
6. Grate your cheese while the egg is cooking.
7. Lift the basket out and sprinkle the grated cheese across the top of the omelette, along with the seasoning.
8. Put the omelette back in the air fryer and cook for a further 4-5 minutes. If you are using a small pan, it may take a little longer for the egg to fully cook, as it will be thicker. Check it is cooked through before serving.
9. When the egg is firm, lift the basket out, and take the pan out of it. Use a rubber spatula to loosen the omelette and then lift it out of the pan and onto a plate. Garnish with additional vegetables if you choose or enjoy it as it is!

Air Fried Avocado Boats

Do you love avocados? These are a great treat that many people love, and if you enjoy them, the great news is that you can easily make yourself some healthy, eggy avocado boats for a delicious luxury breakfast. This is a great way to treat yourself or your partner, and it's one of the more unusual air fryer breakfasts – but still super simple and perfect for beginners! You can easily make this recipe, even if you've never cooked before. Remember that you can alter the vegetables if there's anything you don't like in the ingredients list.

SERVES: 2

You will need:

2 avocados

15 g / ¼ cup of red onion

1 tablespoon of jalapeno

1 tablespoon of lemon juice

Pinch of black pepper

Pinch of salt

2 tomatoes

4 eggs

2 tablespoons of coriander / cilantro

Nutritional info:
Calories: 573 | Fat: 48.3 g | Cholesterol: 327 mg | Sodium: 735 mg
Carbohydrates: 26.1 g | Fibre: 15.3 g | Protein: 16.7 g

Method:

1. Take a chopping board and slice up the tomatoes into fine chunks.
2. the red onion and chop the fresh coriander / cilantro.
3. Dice the jalapeno.
4. Slice Carefully cut your avocados in half and remove the pits using a spoon.
5. Scoop the avocado flesh onto the chopping board. It's okay if it breaks up, but make sure you don't tear the shell. Set the shells aside and dice the flesh.
6. Get out a medium bowl and add in all your chopped ingredients, stirring them together.
7. Juice the lemon and add it, along with the salt and pepper, and any additional seasoning that you like.
8. Preheat your air dryer to 175 degrees C / 350 degrees F.
9. Take some strips of aluminium foil and form them into rings that your avocado boats can sit in so that they don't tip over in the air fryer. Place each boat into a ring and put them in the air fryer basket. Make sure they are stable before you start adding toppings so that they don't get tipped over.
10. Break one egg into each boat, and then place the basket in the air fryer and cook it for about 5 minutes. Take the basket out and check whether the egg is done. It may need a little longer, depending on your preferences and how quickly your air fryer cooks.
11. When the eggs are cooked to your liking, lift the basket out and use tongs to remove the avocado boats. Top with your avocado and vegetable mix and enjoy hot. You can also add some grated cheese if you like.

Stuffed Pepper Boats

If you aren't a fan of avocados but you like the idea of whipping up a fried egg and vegetables in your air fryer, this is the perfect recipe for you! It is super simple and quick to make, and you can add a little spice or cook them plain, depending on your preferences. Alternatively, try them with a little cheese or cottage cheese. They make a very healthy breakfast, and they are ideal if you are trying to cut down on bread or you're going gluten free.

SERVES: 2

You will need:

> 1 large pepper / bell pepper
>
> 4 eggs
>
> 1 teaspoon of olive oil
>
> 1 pinch of salt
>
> 1 pinch of pepper
>
> 1 pinch of paprika (optional; swap for another spice if you prefer or omit)

Nutritional info:

> Calories: 164 | Fat: 11.3 g | Cholesterol: 327 mg | Sodium: 202 mg
> Carbohydrates: 5.3 g | Fibre: 0.9 g | Protein: 11.7 g

Method:

1. Wash your pepper / bell pepper and cut it in half. Remove the seeds and centre, but make sure you leave the edges intact so that the egg won't spill out of the edges.
2. Preheat the air fryer to 200 degrees C / 390 degrees F.
3. Spritz the cut edges of the pepper / bell pepper with a little olive oil.
4. Crack two eggs into each half, making sure that they don't spill out of the edges.
5. Sprinkle the paprika, salt, and pepper on top (or any other herbs or spices that you prefer).
6. Place the pepper / bell pepper halves in your air fryer basket and put them in the air fryer.
7. Cook for around 10 minutes and then check on them. They will probably need another 2-4 minutes, but make sure that the eggs are fully cooked. If you gently shake the basket, you shouldn't see much wobbliness.
8. Take the pepper / bell pepper halves out using tongs once they are cooked and serve them. You can add cottage cheese, mozzarella, or grated cheddar to the top to serve.

EXCLUSIVE BONUS

40 Weight Loss Recipes

&

14 Days Meal Plan

Scan the QR-Code and receive
the FREE download:

Superb Air Fryer Dinners

Your air fryer will really come into its own when dinner time rolls around. The best thing about this gadget is its speed; you won't find yourself waiting for hours for your oven to heat and the food to slowly, slowly cook while you just want to kick back and relax at the end of a long day. Your air fryer is super speedy and will mean you can have dinner on the table in less than an hour.

Air Fryer Chicken Breast

Your air fryer is a brilliant way to make chicken breast, because it's super-fast and simple – much quicker than in the oven. You just season the chicken breasts, toss them in the basket, and fry them until they are thoroughly sizzling and delicious. This is a brilliant way to get juicy, tender chicken breasts with minimal work.

SERVES: 4

You will need:

4 boneless chicken breasts with the skins removed

½ teaspoon of garlic powder

½ teaspoon of salt

½ teaspoon of dried oregano

Cooking spray

Pinch of pepper

Nutritional info:

Calories: 203 | Fat: 4.5 g | Cholesterol: 112 mg | Sodium: 380 mg
Carbohydrates: 0.4 g | Fibre: 0.1 g | Protein: 37.2 g

Method:

1. Preheat your air fryer to 180 degrees C / 360 degrees F.
2. Take out a small mixing bowl and stir together the garlic powder, oregano, salt, and pepper.
3. Spray the chicken breasts on the smooth side with avocado oil.
4. Sprinkle the seasoning over the chicken breasts and then put the chicken breasts in the air fryer with the seasoned side facing down.
5. Spray oil on the side facing up and add a little more seasoning.
6. Cook the chicken breasts for about 10 minutes, until they are starting to brown. Flip them over and cook them for another 10 minutes. Use a meat thermometer to check that the internal temperature has reached at least 73 degrees C / 165 degrees F and keep cooking them if the inside of the meat is not yet this hot. It must meet this temperature to be safe to consume.
7. When the chicken is hot through, take it out of the air fryer and set it on a plate to rest for around 5 minutes. This gives the juices time to redistribute through the meat and prevents them from being lost when you cut the chicken open.

French Fries in Your Air Fryer

If you love crispy chips / fries, an air fryer is the way to go. This is the best way to get chips / fries that are golden and crunchy on the outside and delightfully soft and puffy in the centre. Forget chip pans with dangerous amounts of hot oil and the potential for setting your kitchen on fire – your air fryer is the way to go. Air fried chips / fries are also far healthier than any other kind, and you can get them just the way you like them.

SERVES: 6

You will need:

3 big potatoes
Salt and pepper to taste
2 tablespoons of olive oil

Nutritional info:
Calories: 114 | Fat: 4.8 g | Cholesterol: 0 mg | Sodium: 34 mg
Carbohydrates: 16.7 g | Fibre: 2.6 g | Protein: 1.8 g

Method:

1. Wash and scrub your potatoes and peel them if you would rather not eat the skins (although the skins can turn deliciously crispy in the fryer, so this isn't a necessity).
2. Chop the potatoes into long, thin strips. You can go as fat or as thin as you prefer, but traditional French fries are thin strips of potato, rather than big wedges, and these tend to cook better and faster in the air fryer.
3. Get a bath of cold water and submerge your potato chunks in the water so that they are completely covered. Leave them to soak for one hour. This removes excess starch from the water and ensures that your fries will turn crispy and delicious in the air fryer.
4. When your fries are nearly ready, preheat your air fryer to 190 degrees C / 375 degrees F.
5. Drain the fries and pat the excess water off them, and then toss them with oil, salt, and pepper.
6. Put the fries in a single layer in the bottom of the fryer basket and then put the basket in the air fryer and cook the fries for about 10 minutes. Give them a gentle toss, and cook for a further 3 minutes, until they are golden and crispy.
7. If you need to do more than one batch of fries, put the finished fries on a baking sheet in a warm oven and leave them to rest while you cook the other fries. This will make it easier to get everything piping hot when you serve the meal.

Avocado And Bacon Fries

Do you love avocado? If so, it's well worth trying these amazing avocado and bacon fries, which are quick and simple to make, and are the perfect way to enjoy avocado. They aren't the healthiest thing on the planet, with all that bacon, but they are absolutely delicious. The recipe makes 24, so there's enough for everyone to have two, or one if you're serving up at a party. These are an appetizer that's bound to wow your guests, and they are very easy to make!

SERVES: 12

You will need:

> 24 strips of bacon
> 3 avocados

Nutritional info: Calories:
308 | Fat: 25.7 g | Cholesterol: 42 mg | Sodium: 881 mg
Carbohydrates: 4.9 g | Fibre: 3.4 g Protein: 15 g

Method:

1. Preheat your air fryer to 200 degrees C / 400 degrees F.
2. Scoop the avocado flesh out of the skins and slice each one into eight wedges. Remove the pits as you work; you should get four slices from each half of the fruit. Try to get them close in size, as this will ensure even cooking.
3. Wrap each piece in bacon, trimming the bacon if necessary, and then arrange them in a single layer in the bottom of your air fryer basket. Put the bacon's seam down, as this will help it all to stay together in the fryer. You will need to make multiple batches.
4. Cook them for around 8 minutes, until the bacon is fully cooked and starting to turn crispy. Serve them hot with any dipping sauce you fancy.

Air Fryer Crispy Salmon

If you love salmon, you might be delighted to learn that you can cook it very easily in your air fryer. This will give you crispy, flaky fish full of delicious and rich juices. Serve with some lemon and cream cheese for the perfect recipe and enjoy that crispy crust you won't get with any other cooking method. It's a good idea to leave the skin on your salmon, because this will help to trap the juices in while it cooks.

SERVES: 2

You will need:

2 tablespoons of butter

1 sliced lemon

1 teaspoon of garlic salt

1 teaspoon of chopped parsley

450 g / 1 lb of salmon fillets

Nutritional info:

Calories: 411 | Fat: 25.6 | Cholesterol: 131 mg | Sodium: 183 mg
Carbohydrates: 2.8 g | Fibre: 0.8 g | Protein: 44.5 g

Method:

1. Preheat your air fryer to 200 degrees C / 400 degrees F.
2. Season your salmon fillets with the garlic salt, rubbing it into the flesh.
3. Put the salmon in the air fryer basket in a single layer, with the skin side facing down.
4. Brush butter onto the salmon and top it with lemon slices (add more if you like lemony salmon, and fewer if you prefer a less sour flavour).
5. Fry the salmon for up to 13 minutes (depending on how thick it is) and then check whether it has reached an internal temperature of 62 degrees C / 145 degrees F.
6. Serve hot with a side of peas, potatoes, and cream cheese, or on a bed of rice.

Fried Broccoli

Do you prefer a bit of a healthier approach? If you want deliciously crispy broccoli for the side to another meal, your air fryer can supply it. This goes wonderfully with seafood or rice dishes.

SERVES: 4

You will need:

1 medium broccoli head
1 clove of garlic
1 tablespoon of olive oil
Pinch of red pepper flakes
Pinch of black pepper
Pinch of salt

Nutritional info:
Calories: 53 | Fat: 3.7 g | Cholesterol: 0 mg
Sodium: 60 mg | Carbohydrates: 4.5 g | Fibre: 1.7 g Protein: 1.9 g

Method:

1. Wash and chop the broccoli and shake it dry.
2. Mince your garlic and preheat your air fryer to 190 degrees C / 370 degrees F.
3. Mix the broccoli, oil, and garlic, and stir in some red pepper flakes.
4. Add a single layer of broccoli to the air fryer basket, and then cook it for 10 minutes until it turns soft and delicious. The outside should take on a slight crispiness, and then the broccoli is ready to serve. You may need to make multiple batches, depending on the size of your air fryer.

Lemon And Pepper Air Fried Shrimp

If you love seafood, you can make an amazing air fried shrimp with lemon and pepper, and it's perfect for a fancy date night or a luxury birthday dinner. These shrimps go really well tossed through spaghetti, but you can also serve them with salad, new potatoes, or rice – the choice is yours. This dish is super flexible and delicious and takes very little time to make.

SERVES: 4

You will need:

2 tablespoons of lemon juice

120 ml / ½ cup of olive oil

450 g / 1 lb of raw shrimp (weighed after peeling and deveining)

½ teaspoon of salt

1 teaspoon of pepper

Nutritional info:

Calories: 354 | Fat: 27.2 g | Cholesterol: 239 mg Sodium: 569 mg

Carbohydrates: 2.2 g | Fibre: 0.2 g Protein: 26 g

Method:

1. Preheat the air fryer to 200 degrees C / 400 degrees F.
2. Peel, devein, and clean the raw shrimps, and discard the waste.
3. Cut your lemon in half and squeeze out 2 tablespoons of lemon juice.
4. Get out a medium bowl and add the lemon juice, olive oil, pepper, and salt. Whisk well.
5. Drop the shrimps in the bowl and turn them back and forth to combine them with the juice. Allow them to stand for a few minutes.
6. Line your air fryer basket with parchment paper to prevent the juice from dripping through, and then take the shrimps out of the juice and drop them into the air fryer. Cook for 4 minutes and then give the shrimps a good shake and cook for another 4 minutes. They should turn white and opaque, with a little browning, when they are fully cooked.
7. Take them out of the air fryer and stir them through pasta (or an alternative dish) with the remaining lemony sauce drizzled across the top.

Chicken Fajitas

If you love tortillas and chicken, this recipe is the one for you. It's super simple, but it also packs in some vegetables, and you can adapt it to suit your tastes with ease. The air fryer will make all the ingredients deliciously crispy and succulent, and this meal can hit the table in around 30 minutes – making it perfect for a busy weeknight meal. Don't be afraid to play around with the spices if you find the flavour too strong or add a little sour cream or cream cheese to mellow them out.

SERVES: 4

You will need:

1 large red or yellow bell pepper

½ pound of boneless, skinless chicken breasts

1 red onion

1 tablespoon of chilli powder (reduce this if you don't enjoy spicy food)

1 teaspoon of cumin

1 tablespoon of corn oil

2 teaspoons of lemon juice (or lime juice)

Salt and pepper to taste

4 tortillas

Nutritional info:
Calories: 219 | Fat: 8.9 g | Cholesterol: 50 mg | Sodium: 82 mg
Carbohydrates: 16.9 g | Fibre: 3.2 g | Protein: 18.7 g

Method:

1. Preheat your air fryer to 185 degrees C / 370 degrees F.
2. Wash the pepper and cut it into thin strips. Peel your onion and cut it into strips too.
3. Cut the chicken into ½ inch strips.
4. Get out a large mixing bowl and add the corn oil, lemon juice, chilli powder, cumin, chicken strips, onion, bell pepper, salt, and pepper, and mix thoroughly. Allow it to sit for a few minutes to let the flavours combine.
5. Transfer the ingredients to your air fryer basket and cook for 6 minutes, and then take the basket out and shake the contents around. Cook for another 6 minutes, until crispy and delicious.
6. Use a meat thermometer to check that the chicken has reached an internal temperature of at least 165 degrees F.
7. Warm the tortillas and top them with your fajita mix, and then enjoy with any fresh herbs or spices you like.

Air Fried Sweet and Sour Chicken

If sweet and sour chicken is a top favourite for you, you might be delighted to learn that you can make it yourself in your air fryer with just a few fairly common ingredients. Amazingly, this is another recipe that you can have on the table in under an hour. You can serve it with rice or with pitta breads, or anything else you fancy. Do note that unless you add food colouring, this won't achieve the classic red-orange glow of takeaway sweet and sour sauce, but it will be just as delicious.

SERVES: 2

You will need:

- 235 ml / 1 cup of pineapple juice
- 1 tablespoon of soy sauce
- 100 g brown / ½ cup of brown sugar
- 3 tablespoons of rice wine vinegar
- 2 tablespoons of cornflour / corn-starch
- 2 tablespoons of water
- ½ teaspoon of ground ginger

To make the chicken, you will also need:

- 2 tablespoons of cornflour / corn-starch
- 450 g / 1 pound of chicken breasts

Some people like to serve this with some additional pineapple chunks mixed through the sauce, but this is optional (not included in nutritional information).

> **Nutritional info:** Calories:
> 712 | Fat: 17.3 g | Cholesterol: 202 mg | Sodium: 660 mg
> Carbohydrates: 65.3 g | Fibre: 0.9 g | Protein: 67.2 g

Method:

1. Preheat your air fryer to 200 degrees C / 400 degrees F.
2. Cut your chicken pieces into around 2-inch chunks.
3. Mix 2 tablespoons of cornflour / corn-starch and chicken pieces
4. together in a bowl and make sure the chicken is fully coated.
5. Add the chicken to your air fryer basket and cook for about 5 minutes. Take it out and shake the basket, and then cook for another 4 minutes.
6. In a pan, mix together your brown sugar, rice wine vinegar, soy sauce, ginger, and pineapple juice. Bring this to a simmer, stirring gently.
7. In a bowl, mix the remaining 2 tablespoons of cornflour / corn-starch with the water to create a gloopy mixture, and then tip it into the sweet and sour sauce. If you are adding extra pineapple chunks, tip them in too. Stir well and allow to simmer for another minute.
8. Toss the chicken into the sauce and stir well, and then serve over rice or noodles.

Air Fried Baked Potatoes

Baked potatoes are a fantastic meal and can be paired with any topping, but if you want to make them in the oven, they take a long time. You need to think about your meal in advance in order to put potatoes on, as big ones can take over an hour to cook in the oven. Microwaving them is quicker, but you don't get the delightfully crispy skins – so why not get your air fryer to help out again?

Baked potatoes are a healthy meal, and the great news is, you can have them with any toppings you fancy – salads, sour cream, chopped vegetables, baked beans, cheese, chilli, tuna, and more. No matter what you love, baked potatoes are a perfect base.

SERVES: 4

You will need:

4 large potatoes
1 tablespoon of olive oil
½ teaspoon of salt

Nutritional info:
Calories: 285 | Fat: 3.9 g | Cholesterol: 0 mg | Sodium: 313 mg
Carbohydrates: 58 g | Fibre: 8.9 g | Protein: 6.2 g

Method:

1. Preheat your air fryer to 200 degrees C / 400 degrees F.
2. Take out your potatoes and scrub them with running water. Don't remove the skins; these will turn crispy and delicious in the air fryer.
3. Dry the potatoes thoroughly and stab them with a fork in various places. This will let the steam vent out of them, so they don't explode in the air fryer.
4. Rub the potatoes with salt and oil, and then put them in the air fryer basket and cook them for 30 minutes. Take them out, flip them over, and squeeze gently (using a towel) to see if they are nearly done. If they are starting to turn tender, they should take between 5 and 10 more minutes. If they are still hard, give them 15 minutes longer. The bigger the potato, the longer it needs to stay in the air fryer for.
5. When they are soft, use tongs to lift the potatoes out and place them on a plate. Add whatever toppings you prefer and enjoy hot.

Steak And Mushroom Bites

If you are prepared to put in a little more time to make a truly special meal, these air-fried steak and mushroom bites are delicious. They do take a little over an hour to make because the meat needs to marinate, but they are perfect for a fancy meal or used to top rice. Roast some root vegetables to go with it as another option. You can make your steak as rare as you want for this recipe, so keep an eye on your air fryer and the colour of the meat as you work.

SERVES:2

You will need:

450 g / 1 lb Sirloin steak

2 tablespoons of avocado oil

½ teaspoon of garlic powder

1 teaspoon of kosher salt

¼ of black peppercorn

250 g / 8 oz mushrooms

2 tablespoons of Worcestershire sauce

Nutritional info:
Calories: 482 | Fat: 16.3 g | Cholesterol: 203 mg | Sodium: 1484 mg
Carbohydrates: 8.2 g | Fibre: 1.9 g | Protein: 72.7 g

Method:

1. Cut your steak into 1.5-inch cubes and wash and slice the mushrooms.
2. Get a large bowl and add all of the ingredients. Toss the meat to coat it in the sauce, and then place it in the fridge to marinate for one hour.
3. Preheat your air fryer to 200 degrees C / 400 degrees F. Spray the inside of the cooker basket with oil and then lift the steak and mushrooms out of the marinade and add them to the basket.
4. Fry for 5 minutes, and then shake the ingredients. Cook for another 5 minutes.
5. Use a meat thermometer to check whether the insides of the meat have reached the temperature you desire (see the guide below).
6. Serve hot and sizzling.

> **Steak temperature guide:**
> For rare steak: 51 degrees C / 125 degrees F
> For medium-rare: 55 degrees C / 130 degrees F
> For medium: 60 degrees C / 140 degrees F
> For medium-well: 65 degrees C / 150 degrees F
> For well done: 71 degrees C / 160 degrees F

Macaroni Cheese

If mac and cheese is a favourite recipe in your household, you will be delighted to learn that this can also be made in an air fryer with very little extra work. In less than an hour, you can have delicious, sizzling, crispy mac and cheese on the table, ready for the hungry family to devour. This classic dish is loved by everyone, and it couldn't be easier to make in an air fryer – although you should note that you will need an air fryer-handled for it.

SERVES: 5

You will need:

480 ml / 2 cups of whole milk
4 tablespoons of butter
240 ml / 1 cup of vegetable stock
4 tablespoons of cream cheese
230 g / 8 oz cheddar cheese
230 g / 8 oz dry pasta (macaroni is best but any short pasta will work)
120 g / 1 cup of mozzarella
¼ teaspoon white pepper
¼ teaspoon of salt
1 teaspoon of mustard
Pinch of cayenne pepper
Pinch of nutmeg

Nutritional info:
Calories: 503 | Fat: 32.6 g | Cholesterol: 127 mg | Sodium: 725 mg
Carbohydrates: 30.8 g | Fibre: 0.2 g | Protein: 22.2 g

Method:

1. Preheat your air fryer to 200 degrees C / 400 degrees F.
2. Rinse the pasta with hot water and then drain it.
3. Get a large, microwave-safe bowl and add the butter, cream cheese, milk, and stock to it. Microwave in short bursts until the butter has melted and stir well. You don't need to get it boiling, so it should only take about 3 minutes.
4. Grate the cheddar.
5. Get a large bowl and mix together the mozzarella, pasta, cheddar, nutmeg, cayenne pepper, salt, pepper, and the melted stock mixture.
6. Pour this mixture into an air fryer handled pan, and then place some greased parchment paper across the top, followed by a layer of tinfoil. Put the pan into the air fryer and cook it for 35 minutes.
7. Use a fork to check whether the pasta is done, cooking for up to 10 more minutes if not. Remove the lids when complete, stir, and serve hot.

Lunchtime Inspirations

An air fryer isn't a great option if you're not at home to use it for your lunches, because fried food isn't nice when left to go cold. That might mean you rarely get to use your air fryer to make lunch (unless you work from home). When you do have the opportunity, however, it's a fantastic way to enjoy a quick, easy, and satisfying lunch – so let's look at some great lunchtime ideas you can try!

Air Fried Pizza

Do you love pizza for lunch? Air fryer pizza is fantastic and shouldn't take you long to make – so be prepared to enjoy some stringy, cheesy goodness. Again, this recipe can easily be adapted to include all your favourite toppings, so feel free to adjust it however you like. It's a super simple and fun way to enjoy pizza on your lunch break.

SERVES: 1

You will need:

2 tablespoons of tomato sauce
¼ cup of mozzarella cheese (or substitute half of this for
cheddar if you choose)
1 whole wheat pitta bread
8 slices of pepperoni
1 tablespoon of chopped parsley to serve (or other herbs if you prefer)
Cooking spray

Nutritional info:
Calories: 421 | Fat: 22.9 g | Cholesterol: 50 mg | Sodium: 1273 mg
Carbohydrates: 37.3 g | Fibre: 5.3 g | Protein: 18.8 g

Method:

1. Take your pitta and spread your tomato sauce across the top of it. Leave a small border around the edges; this will crisp up while it cooks.
2. Grate your mozzarella or cheddar and then sprinkle this across the top, along with the pepperoni slices.
3. Lightly spray the top of your pizza with cooking oil and place it in the bottom of the air fryer basket. Cook at 200 degrees C / 400 degrees F for around 6 minutes and then check on it. It may need another couple of minutes. The cheese should be fully melted and gooey by the time you serve it.
4. Lift it out of the air fryer basket using a spatula and allow it to cool slightly, and then slice and serve.

Vegetable And Ham Omelette

If you love simple lunches and you're in a bit of a hurry, did you know that you can make a delicious, nutritious, and simple omelette in your air fryer? The beauty of this recipe is that you can add any vegetables you enjoy, plus cheese, spices, herbs, and anything else you like. This is one of the most versatile recipes out there, and it takes less than 10 minutes to make!

SERVES: 1

You will need:

50 g / 1.7 oz of ham
50 g / 1.7 oz of mushrooms
½ red bell pepper
1 green onion
60 ml / ¼ cup of milk
2 eggs
55 g / ¼ cup of mozzarella
Pinch of salt
Herbs of your choice

Nutritional info:
Calories: 292 | Fat: 15.9 g | Cholesterol: 365 mg | Sodium: 1008 mg
Carbohydrates: 13.1 g | Fibre: 2.3 g | Protein: 25.8 g

Method:

1. Get out a small bowl and crack the eggs into it. Add the milk and whisk thoroughly until frothy.
2. Wash and chop the vegetables into fine slices, and then add them to the egg mix, along with a pinch of salt.
3. Grease a 3 inch x 6 inch pan and pour the egg mixture into it.
4. Place the pan in the basket of the air fryer and cook at 175 degrees C / 350 degrees F for 4 minutes.
5. Toss the cheese in and cook for a further 4-6 minutes, until the eggs have solidified to your liking.
6. Lift the basket out and use a rubber spatula to gently ease the edges of the egg away from the pan. Slip the spatula underneath the edge and serve with additional toppings.

Air Fried Chicken, Veg, And Rice

If you're feeling some fried rice for lunch, this is extremely easy to create in your air fryer. It should only take a few minutes to throw together the necessary ingredients, and you can easily make this vegetarian or even vegan by omitting the chicken. All the ingredients are things you are likely to have at home, and it's easy to make a large portion of this rice to enjoy throughout the week! Note that you will again need a suitable pan for this recipe; the rice will go through the holes in the air fryer basket otherwise.

SERVES: 8

You will need:

25 g / ½ cup of onion
140 g / 1 cup of chicken
525 g / 3 cups of cooked white rice
1 tablespoon of vegetable oil
140 g / 1 cup of peas
150 g / 1 cup of carrots
6 tablespoons of soy sauce

Nutritional info:
Calories: 325 | Fat: 2.8 g | Cholesterol: 13 mg | Sodium: 715 mg
Carbohydrates: 61.3 g | Fibre: 2.6 g | Protein: 12 g

Method:

1. Cook some white rice until done, and then rinse it with cold water and set it aside to cool.
2. Dice your chicken and cook it, and peel and chop the onion.
3. Get a large mixing bowl and add the cold rice to it. Pour in the vegetable oil and the soy sauce, and mix well.
4. Add the onion, peas, carrots, chicken, and onion, and mix well.
5. Pour the rice into a lightly greased pan, and put it in your air fryer at 180 degrees C / 350 degrees F for 20 minutes. You may wish to take it out and shake it occasionally, but it should need minimal attention.
6. Serve hot and enjoy! Store any leftovers in the fridge or the freezer once they have reached room temperature.

Garlicky Brussels Sprouts

Are you on a bit of a health kick and looking for some way to make your lunch better without having to make too many sacrifices? These amazing Brussels sprouts are the answer, and you can eat them as they are for an ultra-healthy lunch option or toss them into a salad or put them together with a pitta bread. No matter how you eat them, these sweet, garlicky, nutty treats will not disappoint!

SERVES:4

You will need:

3 cloves of garlic

¼ teaspoon of pepper

½ teaspoon of salt

3 tablespoons of olive oil

450 g / 1 lb of Brussels sprouts

1 ½ teaspoon of fresh rosemary

50 g / ½ cup of breadcrumbs

Nutritional info:

Calories: 197 | Fat: 11.7 g | Cholesterol: 0 mg | Sodium: 419 mg
Carbohydrates: 21.1 g | Fibre: 5.1 g | Protein: 5.8 g

Method:

1. Preheat your air fryer to 175 degrees C / 350 degrees F.
2. Wash and trim your Brussels sprouts and cut them into halves.
3. Mince the garlic and put it in a small, microwave-safe bowl. Add the salt, pepper, and olive oil and microwave it on high for 30 seconds.
4. Toss the Brussels sprouts into the mixture and stir, and then lift out and add to a tray inside your air fryer basket. Cook for about 4 minutes, and then stir and cook again for another 4 minutes. Stir once more and cook for another 4 minutes. The sprouts should then be turning brown and tender.
5. Mince the rosemary and toss it with the breadcrumbs, and then add the leftover oil and garlic mixture. Sprinkle this across the sprouts and cook for another 3-4 minutes, until truly tender and delicious. Serve hot and enjoy.

Air Fried Asparagus

Following on from the healthy Brussels sprouts, if you're an asparagus-lover, you can also make this delicious vegetable in your air fryer quickly and easily. This makes a fabulous lunch to throw together, and you can serve it with cheese, a side of rice, new potatoes, or stirred through pasta – or just have it plain! This vegetable is good enough to enjoy on its own, especially when crispy and hot.

SERVES: 4

You will need:

450 g / 1 lb of asparagus

4 teaspoons of olive oil

½ teaspoon of pepper

1 clove of garlic

55 g / ¼ cup of mayonnaise

28 g Parmesan

1 ½ teaspoons of lemon zest

¼ teaspoon of salt

Nutritional info:
Calories: 145 | Fat: 11.2 g | Cholesterol: 9 mg | Sodium: 267 mg
Carbohydrates: 8.7 g | Fibre: 2.5 g | Protein: 5 g

Method:

1. Preheat your air fryer to 190 degrees C / 375 degrees F.
2. Wash your asparagus and trim the ends off. Mince your garlic and add this, the asparagus, the olive oil, the mayonnaise, the lemon zest, the pepper, and the salt to a large bowl. Toss everything together until the asparagus is thoroughly coated.
3. Place a single layer of asparagus on a greased tray at the bottom of your air fryer basket and cook for about 5 minutes, until tender and brown. You will likely need to work in batches. When you have cooked all of the asparagus, transfer it to a platter and sprinkle the grated Parmesan across it.

Fried Aubergine / Eggplant Circles

Do you love aubergine / eggplant? This vegetable has been making waves lately, and many people love its velvety, delicious texture, and the silky response it has to being coated in oils. If you haven't got time to whip up a moussaka, you can still enjoy aubergine, but instead, it will become crispy and delicious from your air fryer.

SERVES: 6

You will need:

240 g / 2 cups of breadcrumbs
70 g / ½ cup of plain / all-purpose flour
1 egg
1 medium aubergine / eggplant
¼ teaspoon of pepper
Pinch of salt
1 ½ tablespoons of Italian seasoning
Cooking spray

Nutritional info:
Calories: 221 | Fat: 4 g | Cholesterol: 30 mg | Sodium: 327 mg
Carbohydrates: 38.9 g | Fibre: 4.6 g | Protein: 7.6 g

Method:

1. Get out a shallow bowl and break the egg into it. Whisk well. In a second bowl, measure out your flour, and in a third, measure the breadcrumbs.
2. Preheat your air fryer to 190 degrees C / 380 degrees F.
3. Wash your aubergine / eggplant and slice the end off it. Cut it into ¼ inch circles and place these on a plate.
4. Dip each one first into the flour, then into the egg, then into the breadcrumbs. Make sure that both sides get covered in breadcrumbs, as this will make the slices crispy and delicious.
5. Lay the aubergine / eggplant slices in the bottom of your air fryer basket with no overlap and cook for 8 minutes. Take them out, flip them over, spray the tops with a little oil, and cook for another 3 minutes, until the breadcrumbs are crispy and golden. Serve immediately with a creamy dip or spicy sauce.

Crispy Turkey Croquettes

If you love the crunchiness of breadcrumbs and you're a fan of turkey meat, these crispy turkey croquettes are ideal for your lunches. They are a great way to use up leftovers after Thanksgiving, but they're also a meal in their own right, and you can easily freeze them. The recipe makes enough for 6, but if you want all your lunches for the week sorted in advance, simply toss some of these in the freezer with greaseproof paper between each one, and then get out individual portions and serve hot with baked beans or rice. Kids are bound to love these too!

Note that if you aren't a turkey fan, you can make these croquettes with pretty much any kind of meat, or even fish. Simply swap the meat for the one of your preferences and consider altering the herbs if something might match better (e.g., dill if you are cooking fish). This is a great way to make this recipe even more versatile and suit various different tastes in the family.

SERVES: 6

You will need:

45 g / ½ cup of Parmesan
45 g / ½ cup of Swiss cheese
150 g / 1 ¼ cups of breadcrumbs
725 g / 4 cups of cooked turkey
1 egg
420 g / 2 cups of mashed potatoes (including milk and a little butter for creaminess)
½ teaspoon of salt
¼ teaspoon of pepper
Cooking spray
1 shallot
1 teaspoon of fresh sage
2 teaspoons of fresh rosemary
2 tablespoons of water

Nutritional info:
    Calories: 221 | Fat: 4 g | Cholesterol: 30 mg | Sodium: 327 mg
    Carbohydrates: 38.9 g | Fibre: 4.6 g | Protein: 7.6 g

Method:

1. Preheat your air fryer to 175 degrees C / 350 degrees F.
2. Grate your cheese and mince the rosemary and sage.
3. Take out a large bowl and add the mashed potatoes, grated cheeses, minced herbs, along with the salt and the pepper.
4. Cook and chop your turkey and stir this into the bowl until thoroughly combined.
5. Use your hands to shape the mixture into patties (you should get about 12, around one inch thick).
6. Take a clean bowl and whisk together the egg and water. Put the breadcrumbs in a second bowl.
7. Dip each croquette into the egg mixture and then roll it in the breadcrumbs. Pat the coating down well to make the breadcrumbs stick, and then grease a tray and place it inside your air fryer basket. Add the turkey croquettes in a single layer and spritz lightly with some cooking spray.
8. Cook for about 5 minutes, and then flip and spritz again. Cook for another 5 minutes, so that both sides are rich, golden brown. Serve with sour cream or allow to cool to room temperature and then freeze.

Air Fried Cheese on Toast / Grilled Cheese

This is one of the classic comfort lunches, and it's super easy to make, even if you don't have many ingredients to hand. Forget boring cheese sandwiches; cheese on toast / grilled cheese is in a whole different league, and it's a fantastically simple thing to make in your air fryer. You can throw this together in less than 20 minutes, making it ideal for a quick lunch, and you can also add any variations you fancy. Love a bit of spice? Sprinkle some jalapeños in there. Fancy a salty kick? Try some slices of olive. In the mood for fish? A few tinned sardines make an excellent accompaniment. So, let's find out how to make grilled cheese!

SERVES: 1

You will need:

2 slices of cheddar cheese

2 teaspoons of butter

2 slices of bread

Nutritional info:
Calories: 341 | Fat: 26.8 g | Cholesterol: 79 mg | Sodium: 525 mg
Carbohydrates: 9.5 g | Fibre: 0.4 g | Protein: 15.4 g

Method:

1. Preheat your air fryer to 175 degrees C / 350 degrees F.
2. Put your bread on a plate and butter one side of each slice. Make sure you get the butter right to the edges, because it provides the grease that will make the bread crispy and delicious.
3. Layer the cheese onto the bread, making sure that none sticks out of the edges. If you want other toppings, you can add them now. Mozzarella is a great way to make your sandwich stringy and melty.
4. Stick the two slices together. Place them in the air fryer and cook them for up to 8 minutes, until the cheese is gooey and completely melted.
5. Flip the sandwich over and cook it for another couple of minutes, and then take it out of the air fryer and serve hot. Allow to cool for a few minutes before eating as the cheese will be extremely hot.

Air Fried Mushrooms

If you've got some delicious portobello mushrooms ready to use, your air fryer can turn them from plain fungi into a succulent, rich meal. This recipe couldn't be simpler, and it's a great way to pack in some vegetables. You can eat these with any sauce or dip you enjoy or load them up with a bit of sour cream or cream cheese. If you prefer spicy mushrooms, bump up the garlic and add a sprinkling of chilli powder across the tops.

SERVES: 2

You will need:

4 portobello mushrooms (or other large, flat mushrooms)

50 g / 1.7 oz butter

2 cloves of garlic

2 teaspoons of fresh tarragon

Nutritional info:
Calories: 205 | Fat: 20.3 g | Cholesterol: 54 mg | Sodium: 145 mg
Carbohydrates: 3.3 g | Fibre: 0.1 g | Protein: 2.5 g

Method:

1. Preheat your air fryer to 180 degrees C / 350 degrees F.
2. Wash the mushrooms and set them aside to dry.
3. Mince your garlic and mix it into the butter.
4. Put the mushrooms with their gills facing up in the air fryer basket.
5. Mince the tarragon and sprinkle it across the gills, and then top it with garlic butter (this will melt in the air fryer, soaking into the mushrooms).
6. Cook for 5 minutes, checking halfway through. The mushrooms should turn golden and rich. Serve piping hot with a scoop of sour cream.

Vegetable Kebabs / Kebobs

Do you love grilled vegetables? If so, this is the perfect meal for you, and once more, it's totally adaptable to suit your favourite foods. You can make these with meat if you prefer, skewer a few prawns, or keep them vegetable based. Serve them with any dipping sauce you like – but sweet chilli is a great option.

SERVES: 6

You will need:

3 red peppers

1 large onion

1 courgette / zucchini

1 teaspoon of garlic granules

2 tablespoons of vegetable oil

1 teaspoon of smoked paprika

½ teaspoon of red pepper flakes

Salt

Pepper

80 ml / 1/3 cup of your favourite dipping sauce

Nutritional info:

Calories: 77 | Fat: 4.9 g | Cholesterol: 0 mg | Sodium: 33 mg
Carbohydrates: 8.4 g | Fibre: 1.9 g | Protein: 1.4 g

Method:

1. Wash your vegetables and cut them into large chunks so that they can be easily slotted onto the wooden skewers without a risk of them breaking.
2. Toss the vegetable pieces into a large mixing bowl and add the chilli sauce (or other sauce), garlic granules, paprika, red pepper flakes, and vegetable oil. Mix well until all of the vegetables are thoroughly coated in oil.
3. Cover the bowl and allow the vegetables to marinate for around 30 minutes so that they soak in the flavours.
4. Preheat your air fryer to 200 degrees C / 400 degrees F and spray your air fryer basket lightly with cooking oil.
5. Slot your vegetable chunks onto wooden skewers, alternating to distribute the different flavours.
6. Space the skewers out in your air fryer basket so that the air can flow over them completely and then cook them for 5 minutes. Flip them carefully and cook for another 5 minutes so that the vegetables turn tender and crispy. If you have added meat, use a meat thermometer to check that it is cooked to the correct temperature.
7. Serve hot with extra sauce or some sour cream.

EXCLUSIVE BONUS

40 Weight Loss Recipes

&

14 Days Meal Plan

Scan the QR-Code and receive
the FREE download:

Delicious Meat & Fish Recipes

Your air fryer can create incredible meat and fish, so don't limit it to fried vegetables and things like chips / fries; it can be so much more! You may not think of an air fryer creating phenomenal crispy salmon, luxurious fried shrimp, or superior pork chops, but it can do all of these things and more, so don't underestimate it. Some people view an air fryer as a gadget for making cheap and cheerful fast food, but in fact, it can create some incredibly high end and delicious meals that you'd never know were cooked in a little gadget on the counter. So, let's explore some!

Air Fried Lemon Shrimps

Air fried shrimps are succulent, rich, and delightfully crispy, and they're the perfect way to lend a meal an extra touch of class. Whether you stir them into a pasta dish, serve them as a side, or use them to top a particularly delicious salad, air fried shrimps are a sure win for all occasions.

SERVES: 4

You will need:

450 g / 1 lb of raw shrimp, peeled and deveined

2 tablespoons of lemon juice

120 ml / ½ cup of olive oil

½ teaspoon of salt

1 teaspoon of black pepper

1 small clove of garlic

Nutritional info (not including pasta/other accompaniments):
Calories: 354 | Fat: 27.2 g | Cholesterol: 239 mg | Sodium: 569 mg
Carbohydrates: 2.2 g | Fibre: 0.2 g | Protein: 26 g

Method:

1. Juice your lemon and crush the garlic into a fine mince. Mix the garlic into the lemon juice, along with the olive oil, pepper, and salt, and pour the mixture into a Ziploc bag.
2. Preheat your air fryer to 205 degrees C / 400 degrees F.
3. Add the shrimps to the Ziploc bag, seal the top, and shake to combine. You can let the shrimps stand for a few minutes so that they absorb more flavours if you like, or simply move on to the cooking stage.
4. Cut a piece of parchment paper to fit in the bottom of your air fryer basket, and then take the shrimps out of the lemon mix and place them in a single layer at the bottom of the basket.
5. Put the basket in the air fryer and cook it for around 4 minutes. Take the basket out and shake it, or use tongs to turn the shrimps over, and then put the basket back and cook for another 4 minutes.
6. Take the shrimps out and inspect them. The shells should have turned pink, while the shrimps will have gone slightly white, and opaque. They may also have some slightly golden edges. If they look undercooked, give them another minute.
7. Take the shrimps out of the air fryer and toss them back into the lemon juice, and then serve with whatever other ingredients you desire. They can be stirred through 225 g / 8 oz of cooked pasta if you like or added to a salad.

Air Fried White Fish

If you love the kind of fish that you can buy from your local chip shop, you might be wondering whether you can reproduce this in your air fryer, and the great news is that you can – and it only takes about 20 minutes! This recipe will be popular with kids and adults alike, and gives you access to a traditional meal that many people love. Serve it with peas or sweetcorn and boiled potatoes or mash.

SERVES: 4

You will need:

½ tablespoon of olive oil

400 g / 14 oz of fish fillets (or 4 fish fillets of a size that suits your family)

50 g / ½ cup of breadcrumbs

Pinch of paprika

Pinch of chilli powder I ¼ teaspoon of salt I Pinch of black pepper

Pinch of garlic powder

Pinch of onion powder

Nutritional info:

Calories: 142 | Fat: 2.5 g | Cholesterol: 0 mg | Sodium: 247 mg
Carbohydrates: 10 g | Fibre: 0.7 g | Protein: 17.9 g

Method:

1. Defrost your fish fillets before you start. This isn't necessary for air frying usually, but frozen fish may make your breadcrumbs go soggy before they have had a chance to cook, so it's best to thaw it out. You can do this in the microwave, or by placing it in the fridge 24 hours before you want to cook it.
2. Take a shallow bowl and mix together the breadcrumbs and all of the spices listed above. You can adjust the quantities of any of the spices if you like to make the meal suit your tastes.
3. Preheat your air fryer to 200 degrees C / 390 degrees F.
4. Roll each fillet in the breadcrumbs until it is thoroughly coated, and then place it in the air fryer basket, leaving room between each one. If your air fryer is small, cook the fillets in batches.
5. Cook for around 9 minutes and then take the basket out and flip each fillet over.
6. Cook for another 5-6 minutes, so that the breadcrumbs are thoroughly crispy and delicious. Check that the fish is hot through before serving.

Air Fried Succulent Pork Chops

Pork chops are a super popular meal, and they're also very easy to make in your air fryer. They take less than half an hour, and you'll find that they stay deliciously succulent and rich. You would never know that they hadn't been grilled, and this is a low mess option for making these without getting meat fat all over your kitchen.

SERVES: 4

You will need:

4 pork chops (boneless)
2 teaspoons of vegetable oil
½ teaspoon of celery seed
½ teaspoon of chopped parsley
1 clove of garlic
Pinch of salt
¼ teaspoon of sugar
½ teaspoon of onion powder

Nutritional info:

Calories: 142 | Fat: 2.5 g | Cholesterol: 0 mg | Sodium: 247 mg
Carbohydrates: 10 g | Fibre: 0.7 g | Protein: 17.9 g

Method:

1. Start by peeling and mincing the garlic finely, and then add it to a shallow dish.
2. Preheat your air fryer to 175 degrees C / 350 degrees F.
3. Add the rest of the seasoning and place the pork chops in the dish. Roll them over to coat them in seasoning, and then oil the pork chops and massage the oil in.
4. Place the chops in the air fryer basket with some space in between them.
5. Cook the pork chops for 5 minutes if they are thin, and 8 minutes if they are thick. Take them out and turn them overusing tongs, and then put them back in the air fryer.
6. Cook for another 5 or 8 minutes, and then check whether they have reached the desired temperature. 62 degrees C / 145 degrees F is the minimum safe temperature for pork chops, but you may want to cook them more if you prefer well done pork – up to around 71 degrees C / 160 degrees F.
7. Serve sizzling hot with whatever side dishes you prefer.

Air Fried Chicken Wings

If you have an air fryer, you're not putting it to good use unless you occasionally create some golden chicken wings in it. You can make them just as delicious as deep fried chicken wings, with a fraction of the fat, and all the flavour. This is a great way to make your air fryer beloved by the whole family, especially the kids, and you can really cater to a party if you're organised and you've got a hot oven nearby to keep the batches toasty while you make more.

SERVES: 2

You will need:

12 chicken wings (to serve 6 each to 2 people)

1 teaspoon of granulated garlic

½ teaspoon of salt

½ teaspoon of baking powder

1 tablespoon of chilli powder

Nutritional info:

Calories: 973 | Fat: 64.8 g | Cholesterol: 232 mg | Sodium: 1564 mg
Carbohydrates: 37 g | Fibre: 2.4 g | Protein: 59.1 g

Method:

1. Place the chicken wings on some paper towels and dry them thoroughly. You want to get them as dry as you can before you season them, because this will give you the crispiest exterior possible, so take your time over this.
2. Preheat your air fryer to 210 degrees C / 410 degrees F.
3. Toss your chicken wings into the spices and rub them in to ensure all parts of the wings are covered.
4. Oil the basket of your air fryer to reduce any risk of sticking. You are not oiling the chicken, so it's important to increase the non-stick properties of the basket.
5. Place the chicken wings in the basket, spacing them out so that the air can flow over them.
6. Cook the chicken wings for 10 minutes, and then take the basket out and use tongs to turn them and shake them around.
7. Cook for a further 12 minutes, and then check whether they are crispy enough. If you want them crispier, turn them again and put them back for a few more minutes.
8. Keep them hot in the oven while waiting for the next batch to finish if you are making large quantities.

Lamb Burgers In the Air Fryer

Lamb is often an under-utilised meat, but this isn't because it lacks flavour or texture. Many people love it, but aren't quite sure how to cook it unless they're making a Sunday roast – so why not try these delicious lamb burgers in your air fryer? They are easy to make and you can again whip them up in under half an hour, making them ideal for busy weeknight dinners.

SERVES: 4

You will need:

1/3 white onion I 1 clove of garlic I Pinch of salt

480 g / 1 lb. of ground lamb

Pinch of black pepper

2 teaspoons of olive oil

Nutritional info:

Calories: 411 | Fat: 32.8 g | Cholesterol: 108 mg | Sodium: 476 mg

Carbohydrates: 1.5 g | Fibre: 0.3 g | Protein: 25.8 g

Method:

1. Peel and chop your onion and garlic.
2. Place a skillet over a medium heat and add the onion. Cook gently for about 4 minutes, until brown and starting to soften.
3. Add the garlic and cook for 1 minute more.
4. Place the ingredients in a bowl and add the ground lamb to the bowl. Stir thoroughly.
5. Preheat your air fryer to 200 degrees C / 400 degrees F, and then lower the temperature to 185 degrees C / 375 degrees F for cooking.
6. Shape the lamb into 3 burgers, using a burger press if you have one, and place them in the air fryer basket. Fry for 8 minutes and then take them out, turn them, and fry them for another 8 minutes.
7. Serve hot with bread rolls or boiled potatoes.

EXCLUSIVE BONUS

40 Weight Loss Recipes

&

14 Days Meal Plan

Scan the QR-Code and receive
the FREE download:

Air Fryer Desserts

Many people think that their air fryer is great for making dinners, lunches, and side dishes, but few people remember that they can make some pretty incredible desserts in the air fryer. The oversight may be because we aren't used to "frying" desserts but remember that your air fryer is more like an oven than a frying pan, and that means you can make some delicious treats in it if you get a little more imaginative. These may not be the best way to maintain your healthy streak, but they are fun and can be a great way to use your air fryer more.

Air Fryer Chocolate Chip Cookies

There's not much that can beat a chocolate chip cookie, and if you're a big fan of these popular treats, you'll be glad to know that they are pretty easy to make in the air fryer. Whether you're making them for a birthday party, lunch box desserts, or just for general enjoyment, you can whip up a batch in under an hour, and it's very easy.

SERVES: 12 COOKIES

You will need:

115 g / ½ cup of butter

50 g / ¼ cup of brown sugar

50 g / ¼ cup of white sugar

Pinch of salt

1 large egg

1 teaspoon of vanilla extract

½ teaspoon of baking soda

130 g / 1 ½ cups of flour

120 g / ¾ cup of chocolate chips

35 g / 1/3 cup of chopped walnuts

Nutritional info (per cookie):

Calories: 236 | Fat: 13.3 g | Cholesterol: 36 mg | Sodium: 218 mg
Carbohydrates: 25.7 g | Fibre: 1 g | Protein: 3.8 g

Method:

1. Preheat your air fryer to 175 degrees C / 350 degrees F. Melt the butter in a small pan or in the microwave.
2. Take out a medium bowl and add the melted butter and both kinds of sugar.
3. Add the egg and the vanilla extract, and then whisk all of the ingredients together until combined.
4. Sift in the flour, followed by the baking soda and salt. Stir well.
5. Cut a piece of parchment paper that will fit in the bottom of your air fryer basket, and put it in place, making sure that the air can flow around the edges.
6. Take a teaspoon or a cookie scoop and scoop dough onto the paper, leaving around 2-3 inches around each cookie. You will need to work in batches, depending on the size of your air fryer.
7. Bake the cookies for about 8 minutes. They should turn golden and soft. Lift them out of the air fryer and place them on the counter to cool. Allow them about 5 minutes to cool before serving them.

Air Fried Churros

If you've ever had churros at a street fair, you will know just how deliciously crispy, tender, and delightful these treats can be. They aren't the easiest thing to make at home though – unless you have an air fryer. Because they usually require deep frying to get their golden, tempting dough, not many people make these at home, so yours will be a particularly sought-after treat. You do need a pastry bag with a 1M tip, and the recipe is a bit more involved than some others, but worth the extra effort.

SERVES: 24 CHURROS

You will need:

120 g / ½ cup of milk

120 g / ½ cup of water

115 g / ½ cup of butter

120 g / 1 cup of flour

1 teaspoon of vanilla extract

3 eggs

200 g / 1 cup of sugar, with a tablespoon separated

Nutritional info (per churros):
Calories: 95 | Fat: 4.5 g | Cholesterol: 31 mg | Sodium: 38 mg
Carbohydrates: 12.6 g | Fibre: 0.1 g | Protein: 1.4 g

Method:

1. Place a saucepan over a medium heat and add the milk and water, along with the butter and the tablespoon of sugar.
2. Bring the pan to a slow boil, stirring so that it doesn't stick.
3. Take the pan off the heat and place it on a heatproof mat. Stir in the flour, working slowly so that it doesn't form lumps.
4. When the flour has completely mixed in, place the pan back on the heat and keep stirring it for 2 minutes. It should start forming a ball.
5. Take the pan off the heat and move the dough into a mixing bowl. If you have an electric mixer, the next step will be faster, but you can do it by hand.
6. Beat the dough hard for 3-5 minutes (or longer if you are working by hand). It should start to turn fluffy. This will also help it to cool down; you don't want to add the eggs to a hot mixture, or they will cook.
7. Take out a small bowl and mix together the eggs and vanilla, beating hard until frothy.
8. Check that your main mixture has cooled and then slowly add the egg mixture, beating thoroughly as you stir it. Pause to scrape the mixture down into the bowl every so often and keep mixing until you have a smooth dough.
9. Transfer your dough into a pastry bag with the tip in place, and preheat your air fryer to 190 degrees C / 380 degrees F.
10. Pipe the dough straight into the air fryer basket, using scissors or a sharp knife to sever the dough when you are happy with the length.
11. Use a mister bottle to lightly spray oil onto the churros, and then put the basket into the fryer and cook for around 8 minutes. Take them out and check whether they are golden. If they aren't, give them another couple of minutes in the fryer.
12. Tip the rest of the sugar into a bowl, along with any other spices that you fancy, such as cinnamon or nutmeg. When the churros come out of the fryer, toss them in the sugar and serve piping hot. You can add chocolate sauce if you choose.

Brownies

Brownies are one of the most popular and most loved recipes out there, and if you're going to any sort of dinner or bring- your-own event, you'll find they go down beautifully. They can be classy, but they are also wonderful for kids' parties. You can make a batch in your air fryer in around 40 minutes, and nobody will ever know that they weren't baked in the oven. If you love that crispy top, you'll find this method perfect.

SERVES: 2

You will need:

35 g / 1/3 cup of cocoa powder

¼ teaspoon of baking powder

100 g / ½ cup sugar

30 g / ¼ cup of flour

Pinch of salt

1 large egg

60 g / ¼ cup of butter

Nutritional info:

Calories: 516 | Fat: 27.5 g | Cholesterol: 154 mg | Sodium: 280 mg
Carbohydrates: 70.3 g | Fibre: 4.7 g | Protein: 7.6 g

Method:

1. Grease a cake tin that will fit into your air fryer. It ideally should be about 6 inches.
2. Take out a medium bowl and add the cocoa powder, baking powder, sugar, flour, and salt. Mix to combine.
3. Melt the butter and allow it to cool slightly, and then whisk in the egg.
4. Slowly tip the egg mixture into the dry mixture, stirring as you go to prevent lumps from forming.
5. Tip the batter into your cake tin and smooth the top down with a spatula.
6. Preheat your air fryer to 175 degrees C / 350 degrees F and bake the brownie for 16 minutes. Check whether it is done by inserting a toothpick into the centre and cook for another couple of minutes if necessary.
7. Take the tin out of the air fryer and place it on the counter to cool for 10 minutes before serving.

Air Fried Baked Apples

If you fancy a healthier dessert, baked apples are a wonderful option that looks amazing and tastes even better. These will get even the kids enthusiastic, and they are easy to make. They take a little bit longer, at around an hour in total, but they are certainly worth it, and it's nice to find a dessert that uses some fruit. You can omit the ice cream from these if you'd like to make the recipe healthier or add some chocolate sauce or caramel to make it even tastier.

SERVES: 4

You will need:

1 tablespoon of brown sugar

1 tablespoon of white sugar

½ teaspoon of ground cinnamon

4 tablespoons of butter

4 apples

4 scoops of vanilla ice cream (or your choice of flavour)

Nutritional info:

Calories: 375 | Fat: 18.9 g | Cholesterol: 60 mg | Sodium: 137 mg
Carbohydrates: 52.3 g | Fibre: 6.1 g | Protein: 3 g

Method:

1. Melt your butter in a small bowl, and then whisk in both kinds of sugar and the ground cinnamon.
2. Wash your apples and cut off the tops. Use a sharp knife to carefully cut out most of the core without slicing the rest of the apple. Don't cut out the very bottom of the core; this is going to hold the butter and cinnamon in place.
3. Next, hold the apple firmly and position the knife a few centimetres from the core. You are now going to make a slice that follows around the core, as though you were cutting out a second, larger core – but don't cut all the way through the flesh. Do this twice so that there are two circles cut in the top of the apple around the hole where you removed the core.
4. Next, turn the apple over so that the cut size is pressed against the chopping board. Make small cuts from the top to the bottom all around the apple, being careful not to cut any flesh away entirely. These slices will open up the apple and help the heat to spread through it, ensuring that it cooks more quickly. If you don't open the apple up, it will take a long time to cook and may burn on the outside before the inside is done.
5. Turn the apple back over and brush it all over with the melted butter and cinnamon mixture.
6. Preheat the air fryer to 175 degrees C / 350 degrees F and then place the apples in the air fryer basket with some room for the air to flow. Put the basket in the air fryer and bake them for 15 minutes.
7. Take the apples out of the basket and light squeeze to see if they are tender and cooked. If they still feel too firm, put them back in the air fryer for 5 minutes.
8. Serve with vanilla ice cream scooped over the top.

Air Fried Lemon Cookies

If you loved the chocolate chip cookie recipe, you would find these mouth-wateringly good. They are light, citrusy, and perfect for an after-supper snack. You can add a swirl of icing sugar once they are cooked or keep them plain if you prefer your foods a little less sweet. Feel free to increase the quantity of lemon juice a little if you want it to have a sharper flavour.

SERVES: 12 COOKIES

You will need:

400 g / 2 cups of sugar

230 g / 1 cup of butter

2 eggs

1 teaspoon of vanilla extract

1 ½ tablespoons of lemon juice

1 tablespoon of lemon zest

385 g / 3 cups of flour

1 ¼ teaspoons of baking powder

¼ teaspoon of baking soda

½ teaspoon of salt

Nutritional info (per cookie):
Calories: 387 | Fat: 16.4 g | Cholesterol: 68 mg | Sodium: 245 mg
Carbohydrates: 57.7 g | Fibre: 0.9 g | Protein: 4.3 g

Method:

1. Take out a large bowl and cream the butter and the sugar for 4 minutes, until fluffy.
2. Add the eggs and vanilla and mix them in.
3. Zest and juice the lemon and stir the zest and juice into the mixture.
4. Preheat your air fryer to 175 degrees C / 350 degrees F.
5. Add the flour, baking soda, baking powder, and salt, and mix lightly until everything is combined. You should have a thick, stiff dough.
6. Line your air fryer basket with tin foil.
7. Roll the dough into small balls and place as many as will fit into your air fryer basket, leaving room between them so that they can spread, and the air can flow.
8. Bake them for 5 minutes and then check on them. If they are ready, they will have set firm. They may take up to 7 minutes, depending on your air fryer.
9. Allow them to cool while you make the remaining batches. It may take several batches, especially if you only have a small air fryer. Do not crowd the cookies, or they will run into each other and form into one big cookie, which may not cook very well.

Delicious Chocolate Brownies

If you love brownies, you're in for a treat – because you can easily make a batch of them in your air fryer. These are chocolatey, fudgy, and perfect for any occasion. Brownies make a great dessert, but they also work really well for picnics, fancy meals, lunch boxes, and more. They take less than an hour to make in your air fryer and you'll get 9 pieces from them, which is great for a family, or for sharing around a group. Make sure you have a pan that will fit in your air fryer before you start this recipe.

SERVES: 9

You will need:

- 225 g / 1 ½ cups of 60% cocoa chocolate baking chips
- 75 g / 1/3 cup of butter
- 150 g / ¾ cup of sugar
- 2 eggs
- 1 teaspoon of vanilla extract
- 2 tablespoons of water
- ¼ teaspoon of salt
- ¼ teaspoon of bicarbonate of soda / baking soda
- 95 g / ¾ cup of flour

Nutritional info:

Calories: 267 | Fat: 17.5 g | Cholesterol: 59 mg | Sodium: 166 mg
Carbohydrates: 23.2 g | Fibre: 2.2 g | Protein: 4.4 g

Method:

1. Cut your butter into cubes and then add it to a microwave- safe bowl, along with 170 g / 1 cup of chocolate chips.
2. Gently melt the butter and chocolate chips, taking it out to stir until you have a smooth mixture. Set it aside to cool.
3. In a second bowl, add your eggs and the sugar and beat them together. Stir the water and vanilla extract into this mixture.
4. Gradually add your bicarbonate of soda / baking soda, flour, and salt to the chocolate mixture, stirring as you go. Keep mixing until fully combined, and then stir in the remaining chocolate chips.
5. Preheat your air fryer to 160 degrees C / 325 degrees F.
6. Line a baking tin (approximately 6 inches square) with parchment paper and then pour the brownie mixture into the tin.
7. Bake in the air fryer for 40 minutes, and then insert a toothpick into the centre of the brownies and see if it comes out clean. If it comes out with batter on it or you prefer a slight crunch to the top of your brownies, cook it for a few more minutes. If necessary, cover it with aluminium foil to prevent it from burning.
8. When the brownies are cooked to your liking, lift the tin out and place it on a wire rack. Use the parchment paper to lift the brownies out and set them on a plate, and then cut them into squares and enjoy.

Thumbprint Cookies

If you want a simpler recipe for your first try at baking with your air fryer, these strawberry thumbprint cookies are both adorable and delicious, and they are definitely worth trying. You only need 4 ingredients (although you can add a bit of icing if you want to make them more complicated and sweeter). They are bound to be a hit with the kids and they're super fun to make together.

SERVES: 4

You will need:

25 g / ¼ cup of icing sugar / powdered sugar

6 tablespoons of butter

110 g / ¾ cup and 2 tablespoons of flour

¼ cup of jam of your choice

Nutritional info:

Calories: 358 | Fat: 17.6 g | Cholesterol: 46 mg | Sodium: 123 mg
Carbohydrates: 47.1 g | Fibre: 0.7 g | Protein: 3 g

Method:

1. Take a large mixing bowl and combine the butter and sugar. Mix well until the butter turns light and fluffy.
2. Gradually add the flour to the bowl and mix until combined. Be careful not to over-mix, or your dough may turn crumbly.
3. Wash your hands thoroughly and then use them to shape the dough into a ball.
4. Cover the bowl with a lightly damp towel and leave it to rest on the counter for around 5 minutes.
5. Next, turn the dough out onto a board and divide it in half. Keep dividing the halves until you have 16 cookies, approximately equal in size.
6. Roll each cookie into a ball, and then press down with your thumb to make an imprint.
7. Fill the imprint with jam and continue doing this with each cookie until they are all complete.
8. Line your air fryer basket with parchment paper, leaving space at the top to help ensure the air flows freely. Place the cookies in the bottom of the basket, leaving a little space between each one, and then place the basket in the air fryer and cook them at 165 degrees C / 330 degrees F for around 8 minutes.
9. Check on them after 8 minutes and see if they are done. They may want another 1-2 minutes.
10. When they are cooked, remove the cookies from the air fryer and allow them to cool for around 5 minutes, and then transfer them to a wire rack and leave them to cool completely.

Air Fried Lemon Cake

If you're amazed by the idea that you can make cake in your air fryer, you might want to give this classic, tangy recipe a try. It's very easy, so it's ideal for aspiring chefs, and it only takes about 40 minutes in total – perfect if you're in a hurry and you need to whip up a tasty dessert without spending too much time on it. Be aware that it's not going to be a huge cake, because your air fryer space is likely pretty constricted, but if you're catering for a small group, this should be perfect. It has a wonderful flavour and light, fluffy sponge. You do need a cake tin for this recipe.

You will need:

120 g / 1 cup of flour
75 g / 2 ½ oz of butter
75 g / 2 ½ oz of margarine
75 g / 2 ½ oz of sugar
2 eggs
2 tablespoons of lemon juice
1 teaspoon of vanilla extract
1 ½ teaspoons of baking powder
Pinch of salt

Nutritional info:
Calories: 246 | Fat: 16.4 g | Cholesterol: 61 mg | Sodium: 181 mg
Carbohydrates: 22.8 g | Fibre: 0.5 g | Protein: 3.1 g

Method:

1. Get out a large mixing bowl and add the butter, margarine, sugar, and vanilla extract. Beat together until light and creamy, but do not mix any further.
2. Add the first egg to the butter and beat it in. Once mixed, add the second egg and beat it in.
3. Next, add the lemon juice, baking powder, flour, and salt, and mix until everything is combined.
4. Preheat your air fryer to 160 degrees C / 320 degrees F.
5. Cut a circle of parchment paper for the bottom of the cake tin and lightly butter the edges so that your cake does not stick. Pour the batter into the tin and scrape out the bowl.
6. Place the cake tin into the air fryer basket and put it in the air fryer. Bake for 20 minutes and then insert a skewer into the cake to see if it's done. If it comes out clean, the cake is ready. If not, give it a few more minutes. Make sure it doesn't burn.
7. Lift the cake out of the air fryer and place it on a heat mat to cool for a few minutes. After 5 minutes, turn the cake out onto a wire rack and leave it to fully cool.

Air Fryer Banana Bread

Everyone loves banana bread, and it's a great way to use up bananas that have gone past their best – but did you know you can make a delicious loaf of it in your air fryer? Banana bread is super easy to make and lots of people enjoy it, so it's well worth trying out. Again, you will need a tin or pan that will fit into your air fryer if you want to try this recipe.

SERVES: 6

You will need:

120 ml / ½ cup of milk

160 g / 1 1/3 cups of flour

1 teaspoon of baking powder

1 teaspoon of bicarbonate of soda / baking soda

1 teaspoon of cinnamon

1 teaspoon of salt

150 g / 2/3 cup of sugar

120 ml / ½ cup of neutral oil

3 ripe or overripe bananas

> **Nutritional info:**
> Calories: 410 | Fat: 19.1 g | Cholesterol: 2 mg | Sodium: 610 mg
> Carbohydrates: 58.6 g | Fibre: 2.5 g | Protein: 4.2 g

Method:

1. Get out a large bowl and add all of the ingredients except for the bananas to it.
2. Mash the bananas with a fork or potato masher and then add them to the bowl.
3. Spritz the pan with oil or grease it lightly with butter.
4. Preheat your air fryer to 165 degrees C / 330 degrees F.
5. Tip the batter into the pan and place it in the air fryer basket. Slide it into the air fryer and allow it to cook for 20 minutes.
6. Check the bread is done by inserting a toothpick and seeing if it comes out clean. Depending on your air fryer, it may need 10 to 15 minutes more. Keep checking on it so that it doesn't burn.
7. Allow the banana bread to cool and then slice it and serve and enjoy.

Air Fried Beignets

If you love the idea of trying something a little fancier, this dessert is an amazing one to try. It's surprisingly easy to put together, even if it doesn't look it, so don't be afraid to try it, even if you're a true beginner. You do need an egg bite mould for this recipe.

SERVES: 4

You will need:

60 g / ½ cup of flour

50 g / ¼ cup of sugar

60 ml / ¼ cup of water

1 teaspoon of vanilla extract

1 teaspoon of baking powder

1 egg

1 tablespoon of melted butter

Nutritional info:
Calories: 149 | Fat: 4.1 g | Cholesterol: 49 mg | Sodium: 38 mg
Carbohydrates: 25.2 g | Fibre: 0.5 g | Protein: 3 g

Method:

1. Get out a small mixing bowl and add the egg, water, melted butter, sugar, flour, vanilla extract, and baking powder. Mix them all together until combined.
2. Lightly grease your egg moulds.
3. Add batter to each hollow, filling them to about 2/3 full (the beignets will rise and fill the remaining space).
4. Preheat your air fryer to 190 degrees C / 370 degrees F.
5. Put the egg moulds into the air fryer basket and cook for about 10 minutes. Check on them to see if they have risen and puffed up. If any parts look uncooked, give them another 1 to 2 minutes.
6. Take them out of the air fryer and allow them to cool, and then dust them with some icing sugar / powdered sugar if you like.

Air Fryer Bread Pudding

Bread pudding is a classic recipe that you can easily make in your air fryer. It has a gooey centre, a lightly golden top, and a delicious, custardy flavour. This is a great way to use up any stale white bread that you have around, and it's been a traditional dessert for years. It takes slightly more ingredients than some of the other puddings on the list, but it's not complicated at all!

SERVES: 4

You will need:

8 slices of white bread (around 4 cups once cubed)

55 g / 1/3 cup of raisins

2 large eggs

240 ml / 1 cup of whole milk

60 ml / ¼ cup of double cream / heavy cream

2 tablespoons of melted butter

5 tablespoons of sugar

Pinch of salt

½ teaspoon of ground cinnamon

1 teaspoon of vanilla extract

Nutritional info:

Calories: 293 | Fat: 13.7 g | Cholesterol: 125 mg | Sodium: 301 mg

Carbohydrates: 37.2 g | Fibre: 1 g | Protein: 7.1 g

Method:

1. Get out a large mixing bowl and add the eggs to it. Whisk them lightly and then add the double cream / heavy cream, the milk, sugar, salt, cinnamon, and vanilla extract, and whisk thoroughly until they are combined, and the sugar has dissolved.
2. Melt the butter in a pan and stir it into the mixture while hot.
3. Lightly grease a 6-inch cake tin.
4. Cut your bread slices into ¾ inch cubes, and then spread half of these cubes in the cake tin. Add half of the raisins and top them with half of the egg mixture.
5. Put the remaining bread and raisins in and pour the remaining egg mixture on top. Press the bread down into the liquid so that it gets saturated; this ensures you get a really good texture.
6. Preheat your air fryer to 175 degrees C / 350 degrees F and then place the tin in the air fryer basket and put it in the air fryer.
7. Bake it for about 15 minutes, checking on it occasionally. The top should turn rich, golden brown.
8. Insert a knife or toothpick into the centre to check it comes out clean, and then stand it on the side and rest it for a few minutes.
9. To serve, add a little icing sugar / powdered sugar and some vanilla ice cream if you like.

Tasty Air Fryer Snacks

If you are a big fan of snacks, you'll be pleased to learn that you can make some great snacks in your air fryer. It's flexible and because it cooks so quickly, you can have snacks for all the family without having to spend hours slaving away in the kitchen. Snacks are a great way to keep yourself topped up throughout the day or can be served alongside a meal if you prefer.

Air Fried Spicy Avocado Wedges

Avocados are a great snack to enjoy, but if you're getting bored of eating them with oil and vinegar, you might enjoy these delightfully crispy wedges. If you want to make this treat vegan, you can substitute the egg for aquafaba, but otherwise, it's easier made with egg. If you don't enjoy spice, simply omit the chilli, or if you'd like them to be hotter, add a little more.

SERVES: 4

You will need:

1 avocado

50 g / ½ cup of breadcrumbs

Pinch of salt

1 egg

½ teaspoon of chilli powder

Nutritional info:
Calories: 172 | Fat: 11.6 g | Cholesterol: 41 mg | Sodium: 408 mg
Carbohydrates: 14.1 g | Fibre: 4 g | Protein: 4.1 g

Method:

1. Start by peeling and pitting your avocado, and then slice it into thin strips around ½ inch thick.
2. Take out a shallow bowl and crack the egg in, and then mix it up. In a second bowl, mix the breadcrumbs, chilli, and salt together. Preheat your air fryer to 200 degrees C / 390 degrees F.
3. Swipe each slice of avocado through the egg, and then through the breadcrumb mixture, coating both sides. If there are any gaps, pat a little more egg and breadcrumb into place so that the avocado is completely covered.
4. Arrange the slices in the bottom of the air fryer basket with no overlap, and then bake them for 20 minutes. You don't need to flip them, although you can if you want to.

Cinnamon Sweet Chips / Fries

If you'd like a sweeter snack, these chips / fries are usually a hit. They need to be eaten hot, but they make a wonderful treat for a weekend afternoon, or for a movie night. They are sugary and salty, and utterly delicious.

SERVES: 4

You will need:

2 sweet potatoes
2 tablespoons of butter, divided
2 tablespoons of white sugar
½ teaspoon of cinnamon

Nutritional info:
Calories: 124 | Fat: 5.8 g | Cholesterol: 15 mg | Sodium: 76 mg
Carbohydrates: 17.7 g | Fibre: 2.2 g | Protein: 1.1 g

Method:

1. Wash your sweet potato and cut it into thin slices. You can remove the peel before slicing if you like or leave it on; it will turn crispy and delicious.
2. Preheat your air fryer to 190 degrees C / 380 degrees F.
3. Melt the butter and scoop 1 tablespoon over the fries, tossing to coat them.
4. Put the chips / fries in the basket. It's fine to let the fries touch, but don't fill the basket too full, or they won't crisp up properly.
5. Fry them for 10 minutes, and then take the basket out and shake it thoroughly. Put them back in and fry for another 5-8 minutes.
6. Put them on a plate and sprinkle them with sugar and cinnamon, and the remaining butter. Mix to coat the chips / fries and enjoy hot.

Cornbread

Cornbread makes a wonderful snack, with a delicious, soft, buttery flavour. It's easy to make, especially if you have some silicone muffin cases that can be used in your air fryer. You can also use any square pan that will fit into your air fryer. This only takes about 20 minutes to make, and it's a food you can snack on any time!

SERVES: 8

You will need:

- 120 g / ¾ cup of cornmeal
- 1 teaspoon of baking powder
- Pinch of salt
- 155 g / 1 ¼ cups of flour
- 3 tablespoons of sugar
- 1 large egg
- 55 g / ¼ cup of melted butter
- 240 ml / 1 cup of buttermilk

Nutritional info:

Calories: 202 | Fat: 7.2 g | Cholesterol: 40 mg | Sodium: 160 mg
Carbohydrates: 30 g | Fibre: 1.4 g | Protein: 4.8 g

Method:

1. Get out a medium bowl and then sift together the cornmeal, baking powder, salt, flour, and sugar.
2. Melt the butter and add it to the bowl, followed by the egg and buttermilk. Stir the ingredients together until they form a thick batter.
3. Preheat your air fryer to 175 degrees C / 350 degrees F.
4. Pour the batter into the baking dish or silicone cups, leaving a bit of room at the top.
5. Place the tin or cups in the air fryer basket, and then cook for 14 minutes. Use a toothpick to test whether the cornbread is cooked through, and make sure it is golden brown before serving.

Cauliflower And Sweet Potato Tots

Do you love potato tots? If so, this twist on the classic recipe is perfect and pretty simple, although you do need slightly more ingredients than for some of the other suggested recipes. These are a great treat for kids, and ideal for encouraging them to eat more vegetables. If you're throwing a party, these will go down beautifully!

SERVES: 22 TOTS

You will need:

350 g / 12 oz of sweet potato

1 small cauliflower

1 teaspoon of garlic powder

25 g / ½ cup of onion

3 teaspoons of olive oil

Pinch of salt

Pinch of pepper

80 g / 1/3 cup of cheddar cheese

3 tablespoons of corn-starch

1 egg white

Pinch of herbs of your choice (e.g., basil, chives, thyme)

45 g / ½ cup of Parmesan

Nutritional info (per Tot):
Calories: 43 | Fat: 1.7 g | Cholesterol: 3 mg | Sodium: 145 mg
Carbohydrates: 5.4 g | Fibre: 0.9 g | Protein: 1.9 g

Method:

1. Peel your sweet potato and dice it, and then lightly steam it on the stove for about 4 minutes, until it's starting to turn tender.
2. Put the potato in a food processor and pulse it until it is shredded so you can mix it to make potato tots.
3. Take a clean towel and squeeze the liquid out of the potato. When you have done this, put it in a large bowl.
4. Pulse the cauliflower in your food processor or chop it into small chunks. Next, add 1 tablespoon of water and steam it lightly for a couple of minutes until it is just firm, rather than mushy.
5. When it's ready, again press the water out of it using another clean towel, and tip it in with the sweet potato. The more water you can remove at this stage, the crispier your potato tots will be.
6. Separate your egg and tip the white into the bowl. You can put the yolk aside to use in scrambled eggs or something else, as you won't need it for the tots.
7. Add the garlic powder, olive oil, salt, pepper, and corn-starch.
8. Dice your onion finely and add it to the bowl.
9. Grate both the cheddar and the Parmesan and add these to the bowl. Mix everything together.
10. Lightly grease a baking tray and scoop out a small amount of the mixture and shape it into a potato tot. You can either do balls or cylinders. Do this with the whole mixture, spacing them out on the sheet so that they don't stick together.
11. Place the sheet in the fridge and chill the tots for 20 minutes.
12. Preheat your air fryer to 200 degrees C / 400 degrees F.
13. Take the tots out of the fridge and lightly brush them with oil, and then place a batch of tots in your air fryer basket, leaving a little space between each one.
14. Place the basket in the fryer and cook the tots for about 6 minutes.
15. Take the basket out and use tongs to turn each potato tot over so that the underside can cook properly. Place the basket back in the air fryer.
16. Fry for another 6 minutes and then check whether the tots are crispy enough. They may need a couple more minutes, depending on your fryer.
17. Keep the first batch warm in the oven while you fry the remaining batches using the same method. When you've finished, serve hot and enjoy.

Air Fried Roasted Green Beans and Mushrooms

If you're looking for a healthy, vegetable-based side dish, these are perfect. The vegetables look pretty together, and you can adjust the herbs and spices to your taste. This is a super easy side to make, uses minimal ingredients, and only takes about half an hour to make, so it's ideal for weeknight dinners. The beans really shine in this recipe, so use nice fresh green beans for the best results.

SERVES: 6

You will need:

450 g / 1 lb. of green beans

225 / ½ lb. of mushrooms

1 small red onion

2 tablespoons of olive oil

½ teaspoon of thyme

½ teaspoon of basil

Pinch of salt

Pinch of pepper

Nutritional info:
Calories: 77 | Fat: 4.9 g | Cholesterol: 0 mg | Sodium: 34 mg
Carbohydrates: 7.8 g | Fibre: 3.2 g |Protein: 2.7 g

Method:

1. Wash your green beans and mushrooms.
2. Slice the green beans into 2-inch lengths.
3. Slice the mushrooms thinly.
4. Peel your onion and slice it thinly.
5. Preheat your air fryer to 190 degrees C / 375 degrees F.
6. Get a large bowl and mix all of the ingredients together, tossing the green beans and mushrooms to ensure they are fully coated.
7. Lightly grease a tray that will fit in your air fryer basket and spread the vegetables in a thin layer on it. Thin out any clumps, and then cook for about 10 minutes.
8. The vegetables should be turning tender at this point. Take the basket out and gently stir the ingredients so new areas are exposed to the heat.
9. Cook for another 4-8 minutes, checking every few minutes to make sure that the vegetables don't burn. They should turn golden brown, at which point, they are ready to serve.

Air Fryer Bacon-wrapped Scallops

Even if you aren't a master chef yet, there are some very fancy things that you can make with your air fryer without investing hours in the cooking process. These scallops are the perfect appetizer for any party, and they are also really easy to make. Your guests will love them – or you can make them as a fancy side dish for a date night or a special dinner with your family.

SERVES: 9 (MAKES 36 SCALLOPS)

You will need:

2 tablespoons of Sriracha sauce

115 g / ½ cup of mayonnaise

450 g / 1 lb. of scallops

12 slices of bacon

Pinch of pepper

Pinch of salt

Nutritional info (based on 1 serving of 4 scallops):
Calories: 236 | Fat: 15.3 g | Cholesterol: 48 mg | Sodium: 854 mg
Carbohydrates: 5.4 g | Fibre: 0 g | Protein: 18 g

Method:

1. Take out a small bowl and add the mayonnaise and Sriracha. Mix together and then place in the fridge until you are ready to serve.
2. Preheat your air fryer to 200 degrees C / 390 degrees F.
3. Pat your scallops dry with paper towels and then place them on a cutting board.
4. Season each scallop lightly with salt and pepper.
5. Cut each rasher of bacon into thirds and wrap one piece around each scallop. Use a toothpick to hold the bacon in place around the scallop.
6. Lightly grease the air fryer basket and place the scallops in the bottom in a single layer, leaving a little room for the air to circulate among them. You may need to cook them in batches.
7. Put them in the air fryer and cook them for 7 minutes, and then take them out and check them. The scallops should be opaque, and the bacon should be crispy and lightly browned. If they need longer, put them back in for another couple of minutes.
8. Use tongs to lift the scallops out and put them on paper towels so that any excess oil can drain away.
9. Serve with the chilled Sriracha mayonnaise dip and enjoy.

Air Fryer Bananas

If you want an easy and healthy snack to try out with your air fryer, this banana recipe is perfect, and it is bound to be a hit with kids. You can change the toppings depending on what you have to hand, so select anything you fancy.

SERVES: 2

You will need:

1 ripe banana

½ teaspoon of brown sugar

1 tablespoon of chopped nuts

1 tablespoon of Granola or muesli

¼ teaspoon of cinnamon

Fresh fruit to serve (optional, not included in nutritional information)

Nutritional info:

Calories: 87 | Fat: 2.1 g | Cholesterol: 0 mg | Sodium: 2mg
Carbohydrates: 17.4 g | Fibre: 2.3 g | Protein: 1.6 g

Method:

1. Peel the banana and cut it into ½ inch slices.
2. Sprinkle the banana with the cinnamon and brown sugar, followed by the Granola.
3. Chop the nuts and use them to top the banana slices. Spritz lightly with oil.
4. Place the bananas in the bottom of the air fryer basket and cook them at 190 degrees C / 375 degrees F.

EXCLUSIVE BONUS

40 Weight Loss Recipes

&

14 Days Meal Plan

Scan the QR-Code and receive
the FREE download:

Air Fried Vegetables

If you're trying to increase the number of vegetables that you eat, you might find that your air fryer is a great way to make delicious, crispy, tempting vegetables quickly and easily. It can be a challenge to get more vegetables into your diet, but fried vegetables can be particularly tasty, and they are easy to eat, so they make great side dishes or just snacks.

Parmesan Air Fryer Carrots

If you love carrots, you're in for a real treat with these delicious, crispy, cheesy carrots. These work well as a side dish, or you can make them your main meal if you just want something light. They are simple and healthy, and they only take about a quarter of an hour to make.

SERVES: 4

You will need:

6 carrots

60 ml / ¼ cup of olive oil

½ teaspoon of parsley

½ teaspoon of oregano

½ teaspoon of garlic powder

2 tablespoons of Parmesan

Pinch of salt

Pinch of pepper

Nutritional info:

Calories: 170 | Fat: 14.1 g | Cholesterol: 5 mg | Sodium: 128 mg
Carbohydrates: 9.7 g | Fibre: 2.4 g | Protein: 3.1 g

Method:

1. Wash, peel, and slice your carrots into small chunks.
2. Take out a small bowl and add the oil, Parmesan, herbs, garlic powder, pepper, and salt.
3. Toss the carrots into the oil and swirl them around until they are fully coated.
4. Place them in the air fryer basket and cook them at 180 degrees C / 360 degrees F for 10 minutes, or up to 12 minutes if you'd like them to be really crispy.

Air Fried Brussels Sprouts With Lemon

Brussels sprouts are the enemy of small children, but if you cook them up in your air fryer, they are like an entirely different vegetable. They become sweet, crispy, nutty, and moreish. You can add any other herbs or spices that you like to these, adapting this simple recipe if you prefer a stronger taste.

SERVES: 4

You will need:

450 g / 1 lb of Brussels sprouts
2 teaspoons of olive oil
Pinch of salt
Pinch of black pepper
3 cloves of garlic
2 tablespoons of lemon juice

Nutritional info:
Calories: 74 | Fat: 2.8 g | Cholesterol: 0 mg | Sodium: 178 mg
Carbohydrates: 11.3 g | Fibre: 4.4 g | Protein: 4.1 g

Method:

1. Prepare your Brussels sprouts for cooking by trimming off the ends, removing any tough or yellow leaves, and washing them. Cut them in half and cut any particularly large sprouts into quarters so that they can cook properly.
2. Preheat your air fryer to 190 degrees C / 375 degrees F.
3. Pat the sprouts dry and place them in a bowl. Drizzle the olive oil across them, along with the salt, pepper, and any spices that appeal to you.
4. Peel your garlic cloves and slice them thinly. Set the slices aside for now.
5. Toss the sprouts to coat them in oil, and then add them to the air fryer basket.
6. Cook them for 5 minutes, and then take the basket out and shake it. Toss the sprouts around and put them back in for 5 more minutes. If they look like they are almost ready, add the sliced garlic and toss the sprouts again. Put them back in for another 3 minutes to allow the garlic to cook, and the sprouts to become rich and crispy.
7. Serve the sprouts hot and drizzle the lemon juice across them. If you don't like lemon, consider a swirl of honey, some chilli sauce, or a pinch of nutmeg.

Air Fried Roast Potatoes

Anyone who regularly makes Sunday dinners will know the ongoing battle to create the perfect roasted potato – and your air fryer can help here. If you find that you've never got enough space in the oven and you're always fighting for more room, moving the potatoes to the air fryer is an even bigger bonus, and you'll get absolutely delicious, perfectly crispy potatoes every time. You don't need to do any parboiling either, minimising the need for extra pans and more washing up.

SERVES: 4

You will need:

2 tablespoons of olive oil

½ teaspoon of paprika

½ teaspoon of garlic powder

½ teaspoon of salt

Pinch of pepper

680 g / 1 ½ g of potatoes

Nutritional info:

Calories: 180 | Fat: 7.2 g | Cholesterol: 0 mg | Sodium: 448 mg

Carbohydrates: 27.2 g | Fibre: 4.2 g | Protein: 3 g

Method:

1. Take out a large bowl and add the oil, garlic powder, paprika, pepper, and salt.
2. Preheat your air fryer to 195 degrees C / 380 degrees F.
3. Wash the potatoes and peel them if you like, and then pat them dry and toss them in the oil. Make sure they are thoroughly coated; this will ensure that they get a crispy exterior.
4. Put the potatoes into the air fryer and roast them for 10 minutes. Take them out and flip them over. You might find it easier to tip them out of the basket and then toss them back in to ensure that they are all turned over.
5. Roast them for 10 minutes more, and then serve with extra salt and pepper if desired.

Crispy Cauliflower Florets

Cauliflower is a vegetable that many people find a bit challenging, but it's packed with goodness and if you cook it right, it can be delicious. This is another recipe where you can change the herbs and spices to suit your tastes, and you'll still end up with crunchy, tempting cauliflower in less than half an hour. You can again use this dish as a side, or snack on the florets throughout the day.

SERVES: 4

You will need:

1 cauliflower head
1 tablespoon of olive oil
½ teaspoon of smoked paprika
½ teaspoon of turmeric
¼ teaspoon of salt
Pinch of black pepper

Nutritional info:
Calories: 48 | Fat: 3.6 g | Cholesterol: 0 mg | Sodium: 167 mg
Carbohydrates: 3.8 g | Fibre: 1.8 g | Protein: 1.4 g

Method:

1. Wash the cauliflower and cut it into florets. Include the stems; there is no reason to waste these, and they taste just as good as the heads.
2. Add the olive oil and the spices to a medium bowl and toss the cauliflower florets in it until they are fully coated.
3. Preheat your air fryer to 200 degrees C / 390 degrees F and then roast the cauliflower in it for 3 minutes.
4. Take it out and flip it and put it back for 3 more minutes. Repeat this process until around 15 minutes have passed and the cauliflower is crispy and tender. You can eat it hot or cold, so it makes a great snack for keeping in the fridge.

EXCLUSIVE BONUS

40 Weight Loss Recipes

&

14 Days Meal Plan

Scan the QR-Code and receive
the FREE download:

Satisfying Air Fryer Main Dishes

Of course, your air fryer's true moment to shine is in the making of your main meals. You do sometimes need to juggle a bit, as air fryer baskets can be too small to easily cook a full main meal, but the food cooked in there is worth the extra effort, for sure! You can make some amazingly fancy and some very simple meals by air frying them.

Air Fryer Pork Tenderloin

Pork tenderloin is delicious and ideal if you are serving a fancy dinner, because you can't go wrong with this recipe. You can adjust the seasoning if you aren't sure about the quantities, or swap one spice for another, making this your own. The air fryer is the perfect way to get pork crispy on the outside and tender in the centre. You should use a meat thermometer to check that it has reached a minimum temperature of 62 degrees C / 145 degrees F before serving.

SERVES: 4

You will need:

560 g / 1 ¼ lb of pork tenderloin
½ tablespoon of olive oil
1 teaspoon of paprika
½ teaspoon of onion powder
½ teaspoon of cayenne pepper
1 ½ teaspoons of salt
2 tablespoons of brown sugar
1 teaspoon of ground mustard
½ teaspoon of black pepper
¼ teaspoon of garlic powder

Nutritional info:
Calories: 246 | Fat: 7.2 g | Cholesterol: 103 mg | Sodium: 955 mg
Carbohydrates: 6.3 g | Fibre: 0.9 g | Protein: 37.7 g

Method:

1. Trim your pork tenderloin to remove any excess fat or silver skin. Coat the tenderloin with the oil and rub it in well.
2. Preheat your air fryer to 200 degrees C / 400 degrees F.
3. Mix together all the dry ingredients and then rub them into the tenderloin.
4. Place the tenderloin in the air fryer and cook it for 20 minutes. Take it out and check the internal temperature is at least 62 degrees C / 145 degrees F. If not, cook it for another few minutes until it reaches the proper temperature. Don't serve the pork until it is hot enough.
5. When it has reached temperature, take it out and place it on a cutting board. Allow it to cool for 5 minutes before you cut into it. This ensures that the juices can redistribute themselves throughout the meat and prevents it from being lost onto the cutting board. Spread any juices that do run out over the meat, and sprinkle on extra spices if desired.

Air Fryer Egg Fried Rice

Before you call for your favourite takeaway / takeout, get out your air fryer and give it a chance to shine. Making fried rice at home can be a challenge, and it just never tastes the same – but with an air fryer, you can get that amazingly crispy, lightly fried texture without buckets of oil, salt, and a costly food bill. It only takes about 20 minutes to toss this recipe together, and it tastes just like the real thing.

SERVES: 2

You will need:

2 cups of cooked rice

2 tablespoons of soy sauce

1 tablespoon of sesame oil

1 tablespoon of water

2 teaspoons of vegetable oil

1 large egg

140 g / 1 cup of thawed frozen peas

150 g / 1 cup of thawed frozen carrots

1 pinch of salt

1 pinch of black pepper

Nutritional info:
Calories: 320 | Fat: 14.3 g | Cholesterol: 93 mg | Sodium: 1111 mg
Carbohydrates: 38 g | Fibre: 6.2 g | Protein: 10.6 g

Method:

1. Get out a medium bowl and add the cooked rice, both kinds of oil, water, salt, and pepper, and stir them together.
2. Preheat your air fryer to 175 degrees C / 350 degrees F.
3. Tip the mixture into a round tin and place it in the air fryer basket.
4. Place it in the air fryer and cook for 5 minutes, and then take it out and stir.
5. Put it back in and cook it for another 5 minutes.
6. Beat the egg in a small bowl and pour it over the rice and put it back in the fryer for another 4 minutes.
7. Check that the egg has set and stir in the thawed carrots and peas, breaking the egg into chunks.
8. Cook for another couple of minutes, and then serve steaming hot with soy sauce drizzled over the top.

Air Fried Macaroni Cheese

You need a dish to make macaroni cheese in your air fryer, but if you have one, you'll probably never make it any other way again. This meal is creamy, cheesy, and delightfully crispy on the top, and you can make it in under half an hour. It creates a filling meal that will be loved by kids and adults alike. If you enjoy a bit of spice, try chopping some fresh chili into the mix, or add a bit of smoky paprika.

SERVES: 4

You will need:

200 g / 1 ½ cups of macaroni
530 ml / 2 ¼ cups of milk
240 g / 2 cups of grated cheddar
Pinch of salt
Pinch of pepper
¼ teaspoon of ground nutmeg

Nutritional info:
> Calories: 414 | Fat: 22.1 g | Cholesterol: 71 mg | Sodium: 456 mg
> Carbohydrates: 31.1 g | Fibre: 1.1 g | Protein: 22.7 g

Method:

1. Preheat your air fryer to 170 degrees C / 340 degrees F. Take out a 7 cm deep dish that will fit into your air fryer.
2. Add the macaroni to the dish, followed by the milk, cheese, and seasoning, and stir well.
3. Place the dish in the air fryer basket and allow it to cook for 7 minutes. Take it out and mix it, making sure none of the pasta is sticking.
4. Put it back for another 7 minutes and then stir again.
5. Cook it for another 5 minutes and then test whether the pasta is to your liking. It can have another couple of minutes if you prefer it softer. Otherwise, take it out and allow it to stand for about 3 minutes, and then serve.

Air Fried Crunchy Mushrooms

Mushrooms are a highly versatile vegetable, and they can become an amazing main dish in your air fryer. You may want to add some potatoes or something alongside this, or have them with a bit of toast, but they are surprisingly filling as they are. This is a super simple vegetarian recipe that will let you enjoy a crispy coating without any chicken in sight.

SERVES: 2

You will need:

- 125 g / 2 cups (approximately) of oyster mushrooms
- 240 ml / 1 cup of buttermilk
- 200 g / 1 ½ cups of flour
- 1 teaspoon of salt
- 1 teaspoon of onion powder
- 1 teaspoon of smoked paprika
- 1 teaspoon of pepper
- 1 teaspoon of cumin
- 1 teaspoon garlic powder
- 1 tablespoon of oil

Nutritional info:

Calories: 489 | Fat: 9.5 g | Cholesterol: 5 mg | Sodium: 1308 mg
Carbohydrates: 84.9 g | Fibre: 5 g | Protein: 16.6 g

Method:

1. Wash the oyster mushrooms and pat them dry and toss them into the buttermilk in a large bowl.
2. Leave it to sit for 15 minutes and then preheat your air fryer to 190 degrees C / 375 degrees F.
3. Take out a large bowl and combine the spices and the flour. Carefully lift each mushroom out of the buttermilk and dip it into the flour. Roll it around and then tap off the excess flour. Do this for each mushroom.
4. Dip the mushrooms back into the buttermilk, and then into flour to apply a second coating.
5. Get a pan that will fit in your air fryer, and grease it lightly.
6. Place the mushrooms in the pan in a single layer, leaving space between each for the air to circulate.
7. Cook the mushrooms for 5 minutes, and then take the basket out and lightly brush the mushrooms with some oil to help them brown.
8. Put them back in the basket and check on them after another 5 minutes. If they are not yet golden, give them a further 3 to 5 minutes, and check that they are crispy and delicious. Serve them with any side of vegetables that you like; they go well with peas and potatoes. They are best eaten hot.

Air Fried Scallops

For a fancy dinner where you're treating yourself, you can't go wrong with scallops, and these crispy, light scallops are perfect for a little luxury. Make them for a date night or a birthday, and they are bound to be enjoyed by everyone lucky enough to try them.

SERVES: 2

You will need:

900 g / 2 lb. of scallops

120 g / 1 cup of Italian breadcrumbs

1 teaspoon of garlic powder

1 teaspoon of black pepper

4 tablespoons of butter

½ teaspoon of salt

Nutritional info:

Calories: 823 | Fat: 29.4 g | Cholesterol: 211 mg | Sodium: 1871 mg
Carbohydrates: 51.3 g | Fibre: 2.9 g | Protein: 83.9 g

Method:

1. Take out a shallow bowl and mix together the seasonings and breadcrumbs.
2. In a separate bowl, melt the butter.
3. Roll the scallops in the butter, and then in the breadcrumbs. They need to be fully coated; add more butter and give them a second swipe in the breadcrumbs if necessary.
4. Preheat your air fryer to 200 degrees C / 390 degrees F.
5. Lightly grease your air fryer basket and then add the scallops in a single layer. You may need to work in batches.
6. Fry the scallops for 2 minutes, and then flip them using tongs. Fry for 3 more minutes.
7. Take a scallop out and cut it open to check that it is opaque throughout. The breadcrumbs should have turned golden brown.

Air Fryer Meatloaf

Meatloaf is a family favourite and if you are cooking for the family, it can be a great option that is easy to make in the air fryer. Paired with some healthy veggies like carrots or Brussels sprouts, this makes a balanced evening meal, and it's easy to make. It cooks quickly, and if you've got any left at the end of the meal, you can slice it for sandwiches – making two meals in one!

SERVES: 2

You will need:

1 large egg

60 ml / ¼ cup 2% milk

30 g / 1/3 cup plain, salted crackers

Pinch of sage

Pinch of pepper

Pinch of salt

225 g / ½ pound of 90% lean ground beef

2 tablespoons of brown sugar

3 tablespoons of onion

60 g / ¼ cup of ketchup

¼ teaspoon of Worcestershire sauce

Nutritional info:

Calories: 402 | Fat: 17 g | Cholesterol: 190 mg | Sodium: 839 mg
Carbohydrates: 25 g | Fibre: 0.7 g | Protein: 35.4 g

Method:

1. Add the egg to a large bowl and beat it thoroughly.
2. Crush the crackers and add them to the egg, and then add the milk, pepper, salt, and sage.
3. Slice the onion thinly and stir it into the bowl.
4. Crumble the ground beef into the bowl and mix it well.
5. Preheat the air fryer to 160 degrees C / 325 degrees F.
6. Divide your mixture in half and shape it into two small loaves.
7. Lightly grease your air fryer basket and place the loaves in the basket. Put the basket in the air fryer and cook the meatloaves for 20 minutes.
8. While the meatloaf is cooking, mix together the ketchup, Worcestershire sauce, and brown sugar.
9. Spoon the mixture over the meatloaves when 20 minutes have passed, and then put them back in the air fryer and cook for around 10 minutes more.
10. Check the internal temperature of the meatloaves using a meat thermometer. It should be 71 degrees C / 160 degrees F in the centre. If it hasn't yet reached this temperature, cook it for a few more minutes until it does.
11. Lift the cooked meatloaves out of the air fryer using tongs. Allow them to stand for about 10 minutes before slicing to allow the juices to redistribute themselves through the meat.

Air Fried Mackerel Fillets

If you're trying to include more fish in your diet, you're in luck, because your air fryer can make incredibly good fish. It will create a lightly crispy coating, and deliciously tender, flaky flesh. There are a lot of options for cooking fish in your air fryer, but this is an ultra-simple recipe for mackerel. This is best served with sour cream, but you can omit this if you prefer. Other serving options include a bed of peas, some green beans, or boiled baby potatoes.

SERVES: 2

You will need:

2 mackerel fillets
¼ teaspoon of salt
½ a lemon
Pinch of pepper
Pinch of paprika
Pinch of cumin
Pinch of thyme
½ teaspoon of garlic powder
50 g / 1 ½ oz of sour cream

Nutritional info:

Calories: 292 | Fat: 21 g | Cholesterol: 77 mg | Sodium: 475 mg
Carbohydrates: 3.1 g | Fibre: 0.6 g | Protein: 22.1 g

Method:

1. Rinse your mackerel with cold water, and then take some paper towels and gently pat it dry.
2. Sprinkle salt, pepper, garlic powder, cumin, paprika, and thyme over the fish (lightly oil it first if these do not stick well).
3. Preheat the air fryer to 200 degrees C / 400 degrees F.
4. Slice up the half lemon and arrange the pieces in the bottom of your air fryer basket.
5. Place the fish on top of the lemon and put it in the air fryer. Cook it for about 5 minutes, and then use tongs to turn the fish over. Cook up to 5 more minutes, checking on it to avoid any risk of it burning (different thickness fillets will have slightly varied cooking times).
6. Take the fillets out and serve them with cold sour cream (or other sides).

Air Fried Veggie Burgers

If you're moving towards a more vegetarian diet or if you're fully vegetarian, you might love this veggie burger recipe. It's super easy to put together, very filling, and packed with flavours – so it's perfect for any meal. You can serve this with buns or have it with a light side salad if you want a healthy lunch or dinner. You can make large batches of these burgers, freeze them, and just toss them in your air fryer whenever you want an easy, tasty, healthy meal!

SERVES: 4

You will need:

400 g / 15 oz of canned black beans (drain, rinse, and dry)
1 tablespoon of olive oil
2 cloves of garlic
20 g / ½ cup of pepper / bell pepper
25 g / ½ cup of onion
1 teaspoon of chilli powder
½ teaspoon of paprika
1 teaspoon of cumin
¼ teaspoon of cayenne pepper
30 g / ¼ cup of breadcrumbs
1 large egg
Pinch of salt
Pinch of pepper

Nutritional info:
Calories: 204 | Fat: 6 g | Cholesterol: 47 mg | Sodium: 594 mg
Carbohydrates: 30.4 g | Fibre: 6.2 g | Protein: 8.8 g

Method:

1. Preheat your main oven (not your air fryer) to 175 degrees C / 350 degrees F.
2. Open, drain, and rinse your black beans, and use a clean towel to pat them dry. Next, spread them out on a baking sheet and put them in the oven to dry. This should take about 10 minutes. When they come out, set them on the side to cool.
3. Take a small skillet and warm the olive oil in it.
4. Slice the pepper / bell pepper and the onion.
5. Sauté the onion and the pepper / bell pepper for about 4 minutes, until the vegetables are tender.
6. Mince the garlic and tip it into the pan, and fry for 1 minute.
7. Tip the vegetables into a fine sieve and gently press on them to drain off as much of the liquid as possible. Set them aside to dry.
8. Tip the beans into a medium bowl and use a fork to mash them. You can also pulse them in a food processor if you choose to, but don't make them too fine; some chunks will give your burgers a great texture.
9. Add the cayenne pepper, paprika, chili powder, cumin, egg, breadcrumbs, barbecue sauce, salt, pepper, and fried vegetables. Gently mix until the mixture is fully combined.
10. Split the mixture in half and then half again so you can shape 4 burgers.
11. Preheat your air fryer to 190 degrees C / 375 degrees F and lightly grease the basket.
12. Place 2 of the burgers in the bottom of the basket and put it into the air fryer. Cook for 3 minutes, and then take the basket out and use tongs to flip the burgers over.
13. Cook for another 3 minutes, and then place them in a warm oven while you cook the other 2 burgers.
14. Serve with buns, sour cream, salsa, salad, or anything else you prefer!

Fried Sardines with Chives and Chilli

If you have never had air-fried sardines, you're missing out – and this is another great recipe for beginners because it's easy to make and only uses a handful of ingredients. You can use these as a side dish, but many people enjoy using them as a main alongside potatoes or a light salad. You can take the heads off before cooking them, or leave them on, depending on your preferences. You can use tinned/canned sardines for this recipe if you want but be aware that the oil content will be a lot higher, and that fresh sardines may taste better.

SERVES: 2

You will need:

8 sardines
1 tablespoon of chili powder
1 teaspoon of chives
1 teaspoon of turmeric
1 tablespoon of garlic powder
1 tablespoon of flour
Pinch of salt

Nutritional info:

Calories: 244 | Fat: 11.8 g | Cholesterol: 136 mg | Sodium: 602 mg
Carbohydrates: 8.8 g | Fibre: 2.1 g | Protein: 25.3 g

Method:

1. If you are using fresh sardines, clean and gut them. If you are a beginner in the kitchen, it's best to use tinned / canned sardines so you don't have to do this. It's also much quicker to use sardines that are already prepared.
2. Place the sardines in a medium bowl and add the flour, followed by the spices.
3. Chop the chives and set them aside; they are for serving with the cooked sardines.
4. Preheat your air fryer to 200 degrees C / 390 degrees F.
5. Mix all of the ingredients, making sure that the sardines are thoroughly coated in flour and flavourings.
6. Spread some aluminium foil in the bottom of the air fryer basket and then place the sardines on the foil, spacing them out so that they can cook thoroughly.
7. Cook the sardines for about 15 minutes, and then check on the fish and use tongs to flip each fillet over. Cook them for another 5 minutes. They should be golden brown and sizzling. Serve them with fresh chives or with some spring / green onions.

Air Fried Crispy Honey Chicken Thighs

These chicken thighs are heavenly; they are crispy on the outside, tender and succulent in the middle, and an absolutely delightful addition to any meal. You can serve them with any vegetable, such as peas or sweetcorn, or do some creamy mashed potato as a side. They are also super simple, and although the ingredients list looks long, most of it is just about packing in the seasoning so that the chicken tastes super flavourful. Don't skimp on the sauce; it's the key to saturating this dish with mouth-watering sweetness. Note that if you want to make the recipe with chicken breast instead of chicken thighs, you can do so, but you should reduce the cooking time, or there's a risk that the meat will burn.

SERVES: 6

You will need:

For the chicken:

6 chicken thighs (boneless and skinless, approximately 18 oz)

120 g / 1 cup of cornflour / corn-starch

Pinch of black pepper

¼ teaspoon of nutmeg

¼ teaspoon of ground ginger

1/8 teaspoon of paprika

1/8 teaspoon of thyme

1/8 teaspoon of sage

For the sauce:

2 tablespoons of olive oil

60 ml / ¼ cup of soy sauce

1 teaspoon of ground black pepper

4 garlic cloves

340 g / 1 cup of honey

Nutritional info:

Calories: 693 | Fat: 18.2 g | Cholesterol: 285 mg | Sodium: 904 mg
Carbohydrates: 67.9 g | Fibre: 0.6 g | Protein: 67.1 g

Method:

1. Start by cutting the chicken pieces into cubes.
2. Add the cornflour / corn-starch and seasonings to a bowl, and then toss the chicken chunks in the flour, turning until they are completely coated.
3. Preheat your air fryer to 200 degrees C / 390 degrees F.
4. Tip your chicken chunks in the air fryer basket and cook them for around 12 minutes. While the chicken is cooking, you can start making the sauce, but set a timer. After 12 minutes, take the chicken pieces out and use tongs to turn them over, and cook them for another 12 minutes. The chicken should be cooked at this point. Set the chicken aside until you have finished the sauce.
5. Mince your garlic finely and get out a small saucepan; add the garlic and the olive oil to it. Heat over a medium heat until the garlic is lightly softened but turn the heat off before it starts to brown.
6. Add the soy sauce, ground pepper, and honey to the pan, and simmer the mixture for about 8 minutes. You will need to keep stirring carefully; don't let it foam over the top of the pan or burn.
7. Once the sauce has simmered for long enough for the flavours to meld, you can put the chicken in a bowl and pour the sauce on top. Stir to coat and the chicken is ready to serve!

Air Fryer Turkey Meatballs

If you love meatballs, you will find that your air fryer makes incredible turkey meatballs that are light, crispy, and succulent, without being greasy. You can add these to a pasta sauce if you choose or serve them with a bit of rice and a sauce. Alternatively, baste them in a marinara, slice them into a lasagna, or toss them into a sub. These are wonderfully flexible and will work well in many other recipes.

SERVES: 4

You will need:

2 tablespoons of milk

225 g / ½ lb. of ground turkey

225 g / ½ lb. of ground pork

30 g / ¼ cup breadcrumbs

1 large egg

2 tablespoons of onion flakes

2 tablespoons of minced garlic

1 tablespoon of fresh rosemary

2 sprigs of fresh parsley

½ tablespoon of dried thyme

1 tablespoon of dijon mustard

1 teaspoon of sea salt

Nutritional info:

Calories: 263 | Fat: 10.4 g | Cholesterol: 146 mg | Sodium: 692 mg
Carbohydrates: 10 g | Fibre: 1.4 g | Protein: 33.9 g

Method:

1. Get out a large bowl and add the breadcrumbs and milk to it. Set it aside to soak for 5 minutes.
2. Chop the parsley and add it to the bowl. Add the onion flakes, the minced garlic, the pork and turkey, the mustard, rosemary, thyme, salt, egg, and parsley. Mix everything well to combine, making sure that there are no pockets or lumps of ingredients.
3. Start scooping the mixture out and shaping it into balls of around 1 ½ inches and place each ball in the air fryer basket. You may need to work in batches, depending on the size of your air fryer; don't crowd the meatballs.
4. Preheat your air fryer to 200 degrees C / 400 degrees F and then put the basket into the fryer.
5. Cook the meatballs for 7 minutes and then take the basket out and use some tongs to turn the balls over. Put them back in the air fryer and cook them for another 3 minutes.
6. Use a meat thermometer to check that the internal temperature is at least 71 degrees C / 160 degrees F. When cooked, serve with your desired sauce or accompaniment and enjoy!

Air Fryer Lamb Chops

Do you love lamb? This is a food that often gets overlooked, but it cooks beautifully in an air fryer, especially if you choose your meat with care and select succulent chops. With the right herbs and spices, you will bring the meat to life with flavour, and the air fryer will provide a delicious crispness around the edges of the meat. Lamb chops are easy to cook, and you can throw this meal together in about 20 minutes. Add a little mashed potato on the side or serve with rice, and these lamb chops are perfect for a family dinner! They do need a bit more prep because of the marination time, but the taste makes the wait worthwhile.

SERVES: 3

You will need:

- 570 g / 1 ¼ lb. rack of lamb
- 3 tablespoons of olive oil
- 1 teaspoon of garlic powder
- 2 tablespoons of rosemary
- ½ teaspoon of black pepper
- ½ teaspoon of salt

Nutritional info:

Calories: 337 | Fat: 23.3 g | Cholesterol: 94 mg | Sodium: 392 mg
Carbohydrates: 1.7 g | Fibre: 0.8 g | Protein: 29.1 g

Method:

1. Start by taking your lamb rack and using some paper towels to pat off any excess moisture. If the rack has silver skin on the underside, gently peel this off, and then divide the rack into individual ribs.

2. Take a large bowl and add the garlic powder, rosemary, salt, pepper, and olive oil. Put your lamb ribs in the bowl and toss to coat them in the oil and herbs. Place the bowl in the fridge and leave it to marinate for at least 1 hour.

3. Preheat your air fryer to 195 degrees C / 380 degrees F.

4. Lightly grease your air fryer basket and then put the lamb chops in the base, in a single layer. Space the meat out so none of it is touching.

5. Cook the lamb chops in the air fryer for 8 minutes, and then take the basket out and use some tongs to turn the chops so that the underside is exposed.

6. Air fry for another 5 minutes, or until the chops are as crispy as you like them. Use a meat thermometer to check that the internal temperature has reached at least 62 degrees C / 145 degrees F before serving.

EXCLUSIVE BONUS

40 Weight Loss Recipes

&

14 Days Meal Plan

Scan the QR-Code and receive
the FREE download:

Delicious Air Fryer Side Dishes

Your air fryer is also a great means of making side dishes, so if you're planning a dinner, don't underestimate its usefulness. You can create some inventive and unusual recipes, and many of these can be left to cook while you focus on the main meal. They are quick and easy and make superb sides!

Green Bean and Mushroom Dish

Green beans are delicious, and mushrooms are filling and healthy – so put them together and you get magic in a bowl. This should only take about 20 minutes to make, and it's a tasty side that's a great way to boost your intake of vegetables. You can serve this with pretty much any meal, and they'll steal the show with their crunchy goodness.

SERVES: 6

You will need:

1 red onion (small)

2 tablespoons of olive oil

450 g / 1 lb of green beans

225 g / ½ lb of mushrooms

Pinch of pepper

Pinch of salt

1 teaspoon of Italian seasoning

Nutritional info:
Calories: 79 | Fat: 5.1 g | Cholesterol: 1 mg | Sodium: 104 mg
Carbohydrates: 7.8 g | Fibre: 3.2 g | Protein: 2.7 g

Method:

1. Preheat your air fryer to 190 degrees C / 375 degrees F. Wash the mushrooms and green beans.
2. Peel your red onion and slice it thinly.
3. Slice the mushrooms and cut the green beans into 2-inch pieces. Lightly grease a tray.
4. Toss all the ingredients together, including the olive oil and the seasoning.
5. Put the ingredients on the tray and place it in the air fryer basket, and then cook for about 10 minutes.
6. Take the basket out and toss everything, and then cook for another 10 minutes. The vegetables should turn lightly golden. Serve hot and enjoy.

Sweet Potato Tots in The Air Fryer

If you love sweet potato tots but find that they are often a bit heavy for a side dish, your air fryer may be a great alternative. You can create a batch in a little over half an hour, and these tend to be immensely popular with kids, but loved by adults too. You can serve them with any dipping sauce you like, and they are a wonderful accompaniment to fish recipes, or a lovely side to pair with fried eggs and baked beans.

> ## SERVES: 12 (2 TOTS EACH)

You will need:

260 g / 9 oz sweet potatoes
½ teaspoon of olive oil
Pinch of salt
Pinch of pepper
½ teaspoon of chili powder

Nutritional info (per Tot):
Calories: 28 | Fat: 0.3 g | Cholesterol: 0 mg | Sodium: 14 mg
Carbohydrates: 6.1 g | Fibre: 1 g | Protein: 0.4 g

Method:

1. Wash your sweet potatoes and peel them if you would rather not include the skins in the recipe.
2. Bring a pan of water to the boil and boil the potatoes until they are tender but not mushy. This should take about 15 minutes. If you over-cook them, they will not grate well.
3. Drain the potatoes and allow them to cool.
4. Grate the potatoes and mix in the seasoning, and then shape the mixture into tots. You should get about 24 tots.
5. Preheat your air fryer to 200 degrees C / 400 degrees F.
6. Lightly grease your air fryer basket with the olive oil and then put the tots inside, leaving some space between each so that the air can circulate properly.
7. Brush a little olive oil over the tots and then cook them for 8 minutes. Use tongs to turn them over, brush the other side with oil, and cook them for another 8 minutes.

Cheesy Potatoes

If you want a seriously rich and tasty side that will pair well with almost anything, cheesy potatoes are a great choice. You can use sweet potatoes or just plain white potatoes if you prefer; either way, this dish is bursting with flavour and will prove popular at any mealtime. It can be served with chicken, fish, steak, or any vegetable dish that you like.

SERVES: 4

You will need:

1 medium sweet potato

1 medium white potato

1 teaspoon of thyme

3 cloves of garlic

240 ml / 1 cup of reduced-fat milk

40 g / ¼ cup of onion

125 g / 1 ¼ cups of mozzarella

Pinch of salt

Pinch of pepper

25 g / ¼ cup of Parmesan

Nutritional info:

Calories: 142 | Fat: 4.3 g | Cholesterol: 2.6 g | Sodium: 444 mg
Carbohydrates: 18.6 g | Fibre: 2.3 g | Protein: 8.2 g

Method:

1. Wash and slice the white potato and sweet potato into the thinnest slices you can achieve.
2. Coat a round baking tray with oil and then add one layer of potato around the base.
3. Peel and slice the garlic as finely as you can, and add this on top of the potato, with some of the mozzarella and the seasoning.
4. Repeat the process, alternating the sweet potato with the white potato, and then add the seasoning on top of the layer. Keep doing this until you have used all of the potatoes.
5. Press it down firmly and pour the milk over the top. Preheat your air fryer to 175 degrees C / 350 degrees F.
6. Cover the tray with aluminium foil and then put it in the air fryer and bake it for 40 minutes.
7. Take it out, remove the foil, and use a knife to check that the potatoes are tender. Sprinkle any remaining mozzarella on the top, along with the grated Parmesan.
8. Increase the air fryer temperature to 200 degrees C / 400 degrees F and then cook for a further 5 minutes to turn the topping golden. Serve hot.

Bacon-Wrapped Asparagus

If you love bacon and you want to bring some elegance to your dinner, these simple asparagus spears are a wonderful way to do it. You need to get really fresh asparagus for the best results, but these are easy to make, popular, and very tasty. They also look pretty when served on a plate.

SERVES: 4

You will need:

12 slices of bacon
24 stalks of asparagus
½ teaspoon of oil
½ teaspoon of black pepper

Nutritional info:
Calories: 333 | Fat: 24.5 g | Cholesterol: 63 mg | Sodium: 1319 mg
Carbohydrates: 4.7 g | Fibre: 2.1 g | Protein: 23.3 g

Method:

1. Take your slices of bacon and some scissors and cut each slice down the length to make thinner strips.
2. Cut the ends off the asparagus spears.
3. Lightly oil the basket of the air fryer to stop the spears from sticking and preheat your air fryer to 200 degrees C / 390 degrees F.
4. Take one stalk of asparagus and one-half bacon slice and wrap the bacon around the stalk in a spiral.
5. Place the stalk in the basket and do the same for the other stalks. Make sure that there are gaps between each one once they are in the basket. You may need to work in batches.
6. Roast the stalks for about 5 minutes, and then take the basket out and turn each one to expose a new side. Roast for another 5 minutes, until the bacon, is crispy, and the stalks are tender.
7. Sprinkle the asparagus with ground pepper and serve hot.

Air Fried Tortilla Chips

Anyone who loves tortilla chips will instantly fall for this delicious recipe, which creates crunchy crisps that can be flavoured in any way that you prefer. Forget all the unpleasant ingredients that end up in commercial chips – you're in full control here, and this simple recipe only takes about 20 minutes to put together. If you're serving a buffet or settling down for a movie, these are the perfect snack, and much healthier than crisps/chips that have been deep fried! The recipe given here is for salt and vinegar, but you can easily add a bit of spice, some cheese, or sweet flavourings for a dessert- like twist.

SERVES: 3 (24 CHIPS)

You will need:

½ teaspoon of vinegar
1 tablespoon of olive oil
1 teaspoon of salt
6 corn tortillas

Nutritional info (per chip):
Calories: 145 | Fat: 6 g | Cholesterol: 0 mg | Sodium: 797 mg
Carbohydrates: 21.5 g | Fibre: 3 g | Protein: 2.7 g

Method:

1. Whisk the olive oil, salt, and vinegar in a small bowl until fully combined.
2. Preheat your air fryer to 175 degrees C / 350 degrees F.
3. Lightly brush both sides of your tortillas with the mixture and then cut each tortilla in half and then half again so you get neat triangles that can easily be eaten.
4. Arrange a single layer of the tortillas in the air fryer basket and put the basket in the fryer.
5. Cook for about 8 minutes and then check whether they are crispy enough. Tip them out onto a wire rack and start the next batch.
6. When the chips are all cooked, allow them to cool completely, and transfer them to an airtight container or eat them straight away.

Conclusion

Hopefully, you now have a whole host of great recipes up your sleeve to make the most of your air fryer. This cooker is capable of doing so much more than chips / fries, so let its versatility shine and make use of it for any and every meal!

Whether you are making breakfast, lunch, or dinner, your air fryer can meet your needs, producing crispy, crunchy foods with a fraction of the oil in them every time. Air fryers are a great way to cut back on your intake of oil, and although you will still be using some fat for cooking, you can probably already see just what a difference this makes to your favourite recipes. This is both diet-friendly and wallet-friendly, because you won't be eating and wasting gallons of oil each year in order to enjoy your favourite foods.

Remember that your air fryer isn't just about making snacks; you can cook full meals in there, especially if you are prepared to do a bit of batch cooking. If you do need to cook in batches, use your oven on a low setting to keep the first few batches hot while you finish up the rest. This is a little frustrating sometimes, but it's the best way to make use of this gadget when you are cooking for a lot of people. Alternatively, use your air fryer for the sides and appetizers, and cook your main dishes in the oven.

Don't let your air fryer gather dust in the corner while you sit and wonder what to make. Whether you are preparing a great weekend breakfast for your kids or putting together a fancy meal for yourself and your partner, it is the perfect option. You can make vegetarian food, vegan food, meat-lover food – it's easy to create succulent dishes for any occasion.

Remember to clean your air fryer after each use, as soon as it has completely cooled down. This will ensure that it stays fresh and doesn't take on any odd smells. If you do notice that the basket or the pan have taken on an unpleasant aroma, soak them in lemon juice for a little while, and the fryer should be good to go again!

It's no wonder that air fryers have swept the nation in recent years; they offer financial savings, a reduction in waste, and a continuation of the delicious fried food that most of us have such a weakness for, without the associated health issues. What's not to love? Try out some of these recipes and make your air fryer your new best kitchen buddy.

Disclaimer

This book contains the opinions and ideas of the author and is meant to teach the reader informative and helpful knowledge while due care should be taken by the user in the application of the information provided. The instructions and strategies are possibly not right for every reader and there is no guarantee that they work for everyone. Using this book and implementing the information/recipes therein contained is explicitly your own responsibility and risk. This work with all its contents does not guarantee the correctness, completion, quality, or correctness of the provided information. Misinformation or misprints cannot be completely eliminated.

EXCLUSIVE BONUS

40 Weight Loss Recipes

&

14 Days Meal Plan

Scan the QR-Code and receive
the FREE download:

Printed in Great Britain
by Amazon

15892612R00087